History
of
Washington County Georgia

Compiled by:
Ella Mitchell

Southern Historical Press, Inc.
Greenville, South Carolina

Originally Published 1924

New Material Copyright 2000 by:
Southern Historical Press, Inc.

All rights reserved. No part of this publication may be
reproduced, stored in a retrieval system or transmitted
in any form or by any means without the
prior permission of the publisher.

SOUTHERN HISTORICAL PRESS, INC.
PO BOX 1267
Greenville, SC   29601

ISBN #978-0-89308-730-0

Printed in the United States of America

DEDICATION

TO THE BOYS AND GIRLS FROM 1882 TO 1924
WHO HAVE BEEN TAUGHT BY ME THE
FACTS RECORDED HERE
THIS LITTLE VOLUME IS DEDICATED

That the history of the men and women who made Washington County may be kept for future generations, the Washington County Federation of Women's Clubs have had this book written and published.

The officers of the Federation at this time are as follows:

President......MRS. ARTHUR A. RAWLINGS, Sandersville, Ga.
First Vice Pres.......MRS. MACON WARTHEN, Warthen, Ga.
Second Vice Pres......MRS. JOHN F. TANNER, Sandersville, Ga.
Secretary........MRS. WILLIAM BRANTLEY, Tennille, Ga.
Corres. Secretary..MRS. FRED B. RAWLINGS, Sandersville, Ga.
Treasurer..............MISS LOUISE BROWN, Tennille, Ga.
Parliamentarian........MRS. C. D. HARDWICK, Tennille, Ga.
Editor..............MRS. H. M. FRANKLIN, Tennille, Ga.
Advisory Committee { .MRS. DAN C. HARRIS, Sandersville, Ga.
MRS. THOS. A. WICKER, Sandersville, Ga.
......MISS ALICE SMITH, Tennille, Ga.

Membership in the Federation whose labor of love made possible the printing of this book are the

    SANDERSVILLE WOMAN'S CLUB
    SANDERSVILLE TRANSYLVANIA CLUB
    SANDERSVILLE ROUND TABLE CLUB
    SANDERSVILLE SOROSIS CLUB
    SANDERSVILLE MUSIC CLUB
    TENNILLE FINE ARTS CLUB
    TENNILLE WOMAN'S CLUB
    SISTERS COMMUNITY CLUB
    WARTHEN WOMAN'S CLUB

The Federation acknowledges with gratitude the assistance of the Kiwanis Club of Sandersville, in this work.

PREFACE

In November of 1922, at a conference of the High School Superintendents and the School Superintendents of the Counties of the Tenth District, Mrs. E. R. Hines, President of the Federation of Women's Clubs of this District, brought before the conference the matter of having a history of each County written to be taught in the schools. The motion was made and unanimously carried that such should be done.

Some weeks ago, I was appointed by Mrs. A. A. Rawlings, President of Washington County Federation, and her Advisory Board, to compile Washington County's history, and was asked to make it simple so that it could be enjoyed by pupils in the Grammar Grades.

Realizing that patriotism is fostered by a knowledge of who our ancestors were and what they accomplished, I have endeavored to tell as much as possible in this little book. However, it is a difficult task to put into a condensed volume the history of a County as old as ours, and one so replete with events of interest.

But for the sponsoring of this work by Mrs. A. A. Rawlings and the Chairman of the Advisory Board, Mrs. Dan C. Harris, my task could not have been accomplished. They have been tireless workers, using much valuable time in obtaining facts, and in searching records of the past.

With the hope that what we have done will be found useful, my faithful co-worker, Miss Louise Sullivan, and I present this brief history of our County. We are under obligations to many friends as well as to the Histories of Georgia for information.

ELLA MITCHELL

SANDERSVILLE, GA.
January, 1924.

MISS ELLA MITCHELL
1855-1924
"She Is Not, for God Took Her."
FRIEND—CO-WORKER—TEACHER

MY FRIEND—Whose life passion was to give. She gave with lavish hand beautiful blossoms from her garden, and she gave with generous heart the priceless blossoms of a rare personality.

MY CO-WORKER—Who was a constant inspiration toward high thinking and honest living. Willing to co-operate in anything that would further the interest of the school, no matter how much extra work devolved on herself. She had no place in her theory of life for a shirker. Duty was one of the great words in her calendar.

MY TEACHER—Miss Ella found her life work in the school room. A wonderful work, for forty-three years to influence, with an inspiring, uplifting, ennobling touch, more than three thousand young lives. The finest tribute to her and to her work are the men and women who have gone from her class-room to take places of leadership in state and church. She left the school room to "enter into the life eternal."

This history of the people and of the County she loved is the last gift, the last "labor of love."

MARY TARBUTTON FREEMAN.

September, 1924.   Los Angeles, Calif.

MISS ELLA MITCHELL

CHAPTER I
PAGE
Settlement of Washington County.................. 9
CHAPTER II
Minerals, Flora and Fauna....................... 13
CHAPTER III
Antiquities 15
CHAPTER IV
Warthen 18
CHAPTER V
Sandersville 25
CHAPTER VI
Sandersville, Continued 33
CHAPTER VII
Tennille 41
CHAPTER VIII
Riddleville, Davisboro, Oconee, Harrison, Deepstep...... 52
CHAPTER IX
Slavery, Sherman's March, Roster of Confederate Soldiers.. 59
CHAPTER X
Schools of the County—Great Teachers................ 72
CHAPTER XI
Newspapers, Courts, Ordinary, Banks................. 80
CHAPTER XII
Forts, War Records............................. 89

CHAPTER XIII
Industries and Items of Interest..................92
CHAPTER XIV
Dentists, Missionaries ... .102
CHAPTER XV
Governor Jared Irwin, Governor T. W. Hardwick.......105
CHAPTER XVI
Prominent Men 108
CHAPTER XVII
Prominent Men—Continued 121
CHAPTER XVIII
The Hebrew Citizens of Our County................133
CHAPTER XIX
Prominent Men 140
CHAPTER XX
Men of Washington County Who Have Helped to Make It Famous 146
CHAPTER XXI
Prominent Women 154
CHAPTER XXII
Federated Clubs 160
CHAPTER XXIII
Improved Conditions in the County................168
Conclusion 171

CHAPTER I.

Original Location. In 1783, when Benjamin Franklin and others went to Paris to sign the Treaty of Peace with England and George Washington was President of the Colonial Congress, the Assembly of Georgia divided that immense territory from Liberty County northward to the mountains into two portions, one to be named Washington, the other Franklin, in honor of General George Washington and Benjamin Franklin.

Early in 1784, the demarcation of Washington County was made: "All that land lying between the Oconee and the Ogeechee Rivers, from Liberty County on the South to the Cherokee nation on the North."

Settlement of Washington County. Washington County was the ninth county in the State. The purpose of its being formed was to give homes to Patriots who offered themselves and all they possessed in the defense of Georgia during the Revolution. Soldiers from the Carolinas and Virginia, besides men direct from Ireland and Scotland aided in driving the British and their sympathizers, the Tories, from the then sparsely settled territory of Georgia.

Grants of 250 acres were issued to all soldiers who desired to settle in Washington County. This land was to be free from taxation for a period of years.

Much of this land was of the best quality and many people came to make homes. The long list of grants found in White's and Smith's history of Georgia does not show the settlers alone, but names of many who never came at all, but sold their grants. Those who really took up their grants in 1786-1787 were: Alexander Irwin, William Johnson, Jared Irwin, William Irwin, Elisha Williams, John Rutherford, Jacob Dennard, J. Bedingfield, P. Franklin, A. Sinquefield, Joseph Avant, John Sheppard, John Thomas, John Daniel, John Martin, B. Tennille, J. Burney, Hugh Lawson, M. Saunders, George Galphin, Jacob Dennis, J. Nutte, D. Wood, W. Warthen, Jacob Kelley, William May, Robert Wicker, Col. Francis Tennille.

Many of the first settlers were of Scotch origin. These came from North Carolina. However, there were settlers from Burke, Effingham, and Wilkes Counties and a few from Virginia.

Representatives to Convention. Georgia ratified the Constitution early in 1778. Washington County's representatives in the Convention were Jared Irwin and John Watts. While they were in session, they revised the State Constitution.

The representatives in 1786 were: David Gresham, John Watts, William Grier, William Daniel, Thomas Bush, Robert Christmass, Abraham Barnett, Hugh Irwin, Andrew Irwin, and Thomas Harris.

Another Convention of the Legislature was called in 1794 to revise the Constitution which was drawn up in the spring of 1795. The representatives from Washington County were John Rutherford, George Franklin and R. Wilkinson.

In 1798 the largest and ablest Convention that had at that time assembled met, its purpose being another revision of the Constitution. In this Convention were John Watts, George Franklin and Jared Irwin from Washington County.

For Twenty Years after the settlement of Washington, there was little to induce wealthy people to immigrate to it, but the land was so cheap and so fertile that those, who came into the woods poor, soon became independent and were rich in flocks and herds. There was no market nearer than Augusta. However, there was but little to be bought and but little to be sold. The houses were log cabins and the people were chiefly dependent on their own labor.

Cotton Raising. After the invention of the cotton gin, one was brought to the county and cotton planting began on a considerable scale, then a tide of settlers came rushing in. Many brought slaves with them and opened large plantations. This was true, however, only of the rich lands, as much of the county was in pine woods and settled by poor people.

New Counties. The immense area of Washington was gradually diminished by different counties being made from it, among them Greene, Montgomery, Johnson, a part of Hancock, Laurens, Jefferson, Glascock, Baldwin, and Oglethorpe, but the account that we now give refers only to that part which now bears the name. It is very nearly in the center of the State and is still one of the large counties, containing 680 square miles. The population is 28,147.

Location and Topography. Its altitude is 540 feet above sea level. It lies between $32\frac{1}{2}$ and $33\frac{1}{2}$ north latitude and between $82\frac{1}{2}$ and $83\frac{1}{2}$ west longitude. It is bounded north by Hancock and Glascock, east by Jefferson, south by Johnson, west by Wilkinson and Baldwin. Its shape is an irregular pentagon. It is well watered by the Oconee in the west and southwest, the Ogeechee east, the Ohoopee south. Large creeks are tributary to the rivers, among them Buffalo, Keg Creek and Williamson's Swamp Creek, Buckeye, Lamar, and others. The relief is from level to rugged. The soil is rotten limestone, clay, grey and sandy loam.

CHAPTER II.

Among Minerals found in our county are opals, hornblende, flint, agate, chalcedony, marl, talc, and a very valuable burrstone. White says: "There is no region of Georgia more interesting geologically considered than Washington County."

Kaolin is found in great quantities in the western part of the county. It is of the finest variety, said by leading chemists and geologists to be as fine as the best of English clay and of a finer grade than the celebrated Pike's Peak Kaolin. It is in such large strata that it is almost inexhaustible. On digging a well on one of Dr. Hollifield's places, the men had to dig through a layer sixteen feet deep. When the Government and State highway roads are built, the owners of that land will be independent of boll weevils.

Gritless White Chalk is found in several sections of the county that under the microscope shows myriads of tiny shells. This is used in fulling cloth. It makes excellent crayons.

Flora and Fauna. Washington County is second to none in its hard woods, certainly it leads in production of pine and other soft woods.

Of native blossoming shrubs we have a great variety, the azalea, honey suckle, laurel, sweet shrub, elder, alder, nudiflora are a few; then the flowering trees, old man's greybeard, dog wood, red bud, tulip tree, maple, magnolia and bay are known by every one; and the flowers, violets, phlox, verbena, eglantine, sensitive plant and myriads of others.

Audubon says there are 373 species of birds in Georgia, many of which were with us all the time until of recent years they were so slaughtered that many kinds have been exterminated. In a garden and around a home where birds are not allowed to be molested, it is an easy matter to count a dozen varieties, and all of them, save the English sparrow, friends of ours.

When our forefathers came here, they found not only wild savages, but bears, wolves, wild cats, cougars, and skunks, then the deer, fox, weasel, mink, otter, squirrel, rabbit, beaver, and of course, rats and mice too. Snakes of many kinds abounded, the most deadly were the rattlesnake, copperhead, adder and water moccasins, lizards, frogs and toads were abundant.

In the water courses were all kinds of fresh water fish. The Ogeechee was famous for shad. There were turtles and terrapins. Sometimes in the Oconee and Ogeechee were seen the dreaded alligator.

CHAPTER III.

Antiquities. Our county is rich in traditionary lore from the stories of Indian raids, to the mounds found in different sections of the county. It is difficult for children of this generation to imagine that where our towns and farms now stand once there were dense woods, the home of fierce wild animals, and worse still, skulking savages. In the vicinity of Davisboro lived a cruel tribe of Indians. One day the father of a white family went to Saunders Cross Roads (Sandersville) to trade. On his return he found his home in ashes, his wife and children dead, scalped.

I remember an old lady who lived in Sandersville when I was a little girl. She had been scalped in the raid made by the Indians on the border of Baldwin and Washington. For a wonder, though left by the savages as dead, she survived and lived to be very old. What attracted us children was that she always wore a cap to hide the fact that she had no hair.

The Lime Sinks was quite a show place eighty years ago. Then there were lime biscuits, really star fish that had been petrified, sharks' teeth, deep-sea shells, all to prove that this section had been raised by some convulsion of nature and had become dry land. As late as 1875, the place was very attractive, a wooded pathway led from Sandersville to the Sinks or Caves, great oaks, black gums, sweet gums, and hickory trees grew on the tops of the caves. Within were miniature stalactites, a few stalagmites and many shells. Mr. Joseph LeConte, the great scientist, visited these peculiar formations and those that lie to the west of Tennille. The property on which were these curiosities changed hands several times after the war. It was all cleared and now nothing of much interest remains. One geologist has said that the Lime Sinks near Sandersville are the terminus of the Mammoth Cave in Kentucky, that a ridge of limestone can be traced directly through to the caves there.

Just before the outbreak of the War Between the States, lime of an excellent quality was burnt at the Lime Sinks near Sandersville and also near Sun Hill. The lime used in the construction of the Court House that was burned in Sherman's raid was made near Sandersville. The kiln was in excellent condition as late as 1870.

Fine mineral springs are located in our county. In White's history is mentioned one near Williamson Swamp. The water from the artesian wells in both Davisboro and Sun Hill is strongly impregnated with iron and sulphur. Brooks' Spring is asserted by certain chemists to contain nearly, if not all the elements that make Indian Springs famous.

CHAPTER IV.

WARTHEN

The First Court in Washington County was held near Warthen at the home of a Mr. Benjamin Tennille. Soon it was decided that a County Site should be fixed.

County Site. In 1796, a Mr. Saunders, one of the first settlers owned a large tract of land, which included the site or spot selected for the county lot. It was near the center of the county in the oak woods. It was first called Saunder's Cross Roads, because Mr. Saunders operated a store where the roads cross at the corner now occupied by Sandersville Drug Co. The name was soon changed to Sandersville. At first the town grew slowly. It is situated on a ridge between the Oconee and Ogeechee Rivers, 480 feet above sea level. It was incorporated in 1812, and by an Act of the Legislature it had an academy. This academy was endowed by the State with an income from one thousand acres of land and afterwards by an annual appropriation.

New Settlers. From the time it was incorporated, many new settlers came from different parts of the

WASHINGTON COUNTY, GA. 19

country, among them physicians, lawyers, merchants, and mechanics. There was a great influx of settlers, among them the Brooks, the Burnetts, Bells, Joiners, Barksdales, Brantleys, Bullards, Rawlings, Cullens, Davis, Flukers, Harris, Kelleys, Robinsons, Sparks, Smiths, Tuckers, Wickers, Walters. As early as 1804, the stage road was extended from Louisville to the new capitol in Milledgeville. This road had at stated intervals stations or relay houses. Sandersville was the station to the west of Louisville.

Washington Hall. Another relay was established one and one-half miles on the Washington side of the county line between Baldwin and Washington. The Inn was named "Washington Hall." Up to sixty years ago, this house stood somewhat removed from the road. Over the gateway was an arch bearing the name of the Inn, beneath this was the name of the proprietor, David Grier. Mr. Grier was the grandfather of Judge Robert L. Rodgers, a well known writer. At this Inn, many notables were entertained, among them Governors George M. Troup, Lumpkin, Gilmer, McDonald, Crawford, Towne, Cobb, Johnson, Judge McPherson, Judge Berrien and others.

Education. In the early days of the county, camp grounds and academies were established by the Legislature. As early as 1830, there were incorporated four academies in the county, Bethlehem, Davisboro, Union, and Gum Spring. By legislative act, a causeway was built over Buffalo Creek. From the earliest settlement of the county there was an Indian trail that passed through it near Poplar Springs Church. This road began in the Cherokee nation and extended to South Georgia without once crossing a water course. There is still in the section of the county near Warthen a road that bears the name of Indian Trail.

The land on which Warthen stands was granted to **Robert Wicker** in 1787. He was the great grandfather of Mr. George D. Warthen and his brothers and sisters.

The Warthens came from Maryland and took up claims between the Big Ogeechee and the Little Ogeechee. Richard Warthen, the pioneer, built at what is now Hamburg, the first mill in the County. Near the Shoals was a trading post, to which came all the Indians on both sides of the river. The place was named Georgetown. Warthen lay on one of those trails which led through this section to North Georgia.

First Jail. Very soon after the laying out of Washington County, it was found necessary to have a court ground. The place selected was a settlement that had been begun by the grandfather of Richard and Thomas Jefferson Warthen. Already it had been named for the landed proprietor, Warthen. From that time, until 1796, Court sat there. A small jail of hewn logs was built. This quaint building still stands.

In 1804, the notorious Col. Aaron Burr spent one night in the jail. He was under a military guard of United States troops. They were en route from New Orleans to Richmond, Va., where Aaron Burr was to be tried for treason. Just before night-fall the party reached Warthen, the troopers placed their prisoner in jail, detailed sentries, then the others spent the night in the home of Richard Warthen, Esq.

Growth. From a small village, Warthen has grown to be one of the important towns in this section. It has a large trade in cotton. The Georgia & Florida Railroad passes through the town; there are several stores, a bank, and a large warehouse. The homes are attractive and well kept. The school is a graded one, including a High School and a Music Department.

There are two churches, a Methodist and a Baptist. The Baptist Church, Bethlehem, is one of the oldest churches in this part of the State. It was organized in 1791. The Academy of Bethlehem was chartered by the State in 1832.

Warthen has ever been noted for its hospitable homes. The stranger within its gates always feels a cordial welcome. The women of Warthen are very progressive. The Georgia Federation of Women's Clubs is well organized and is one of the best clubs in the county.

Jefferson Davis. An interesting bit of history is that Jefferson Davis, the President of the Confederacy, and his escort camped on the outskirts of Warthen, when trying to reach Mobile to escape arrest by the Federal soldiers. He hoped to get passage to Cuba, thence to Europe.

MASONIC TEMPLE

CHAPTER V.

SANDERSVILLE

Although selected as the county site in 1796, Sandersville remained a small village for a number of years. In fact, until after the War Between the States it did not grow very much. There were a few handsome houses, the homes of wealthy citizens, but the majority of the dwellings were small unpainted structures.

The First Court House, Masonic Temple, and the hotel were of brick. All three were erected after the fire of 1855, which almost swept the town out of existence.

Central of Georgia Railroad. The great mistake made by the inhabitants was the determination that the Central of Georgia Railroad should not come through the town. Therefore it skirted Sandersville and made Tennille a station instead. Had the people given a right of way and encouraged the promoters to come through, unquestionably the town would have increased ten-fold in importance.

Short Line R. R. Until 1875, when Mr. C. R. Pringle, Col. R. Lee Warthen, Dr. H. N. Hollifield,

Judge R. L. Rodgers, Mr. E. A. Sullivan, and others advocated a short line connecting Sandersville with Tennille, the only means of transportation was a hack line for passengers. Express and freight were conveyed by wagons. The short line began where the east lawn of the Baptist Church now is, and ended in Tennille, going down the middle of Harris Street until it turned to the left just below the Carter home, now owned by Jeff A. Irwin, Sr.

There were the blowing of whistles, ringing of bells and shouts of men and boys when the engine came over from Tennille the first time. Judge Rodgers stood on the boiler and made the dedicatory speech. After some years, the stock holders sold it to the Augusta Southern. Then Mr. Louis Cohen built the Sandersville & Tennille Railroad that now exists and that comes into town near the cotton warehouses.

Major William Hodges owned much of the land Sandersville is built upon. He cut it up into lots, sold them cheap in order to attract settlers. The Northeastern part of the present town was all under water as late as 1862. It was called Hodges Pond. Major Hodges' son-in-law, Captain Ben Jones, had it drained and after the war it was sold to different purchasers.

A second fire was prevented by **Rev. James D. Anthony** and **Dr. James R. Smith**, Methodist ministers, who prevailed upon Gen. W. T. Sherman to spare the town, even after he had given the order to apply the torch. The Court House, jail, and factory, a large building that manufactured saddletrees and buckets for the Confederacy, were all burned.

Sherman's Raid. Much has been said about the suffering for food during the war. Neither Sandersville, Tennille nor the county had a shortage of good, wholesome food until after Sherman's raid. It is true that tea, and sometimes sugar, could not be procured, but wheat, corn, and rye were abundant. There were milk, butter, chickens, eggs, hog meat (both fresh and cured), beef and mutton all of excellent quality. On the plantation, the negroes worked under the direction of the mistress to supply the home needs, and to furnish food for their masters at the front. But after November, 1864, when Sherman and his horde swooped down upon the county, that portion through which his 15,000 troops, besides stragglers marched, there was nothing left—absolutely nothing.

Then there was suffering; black and white, bond and free, felt the pangs of hunger and knew want.

Conditions were bad for five years—no cotton left, gin houses burned, country homes destroyed, all animals killed, no implements left, no seed. People as a rule are helpful to those in need, so in the strenuous days of Reconstruction, those who had shared with those who had not, and in a few years, hard times passed away, and Sandersville and Washington County began to prosper.

Open Barrooms Abolished. In Reconstruction days and down to 1886, Sandersville was handicapped by the curse of open barrooms. Drunken men lay upon the streets, rows were of daily occurrence, there was always danger of pistol duels, no woman or girl was supposed to be on the streets on Saturdays or court days, unless protected by some man, no woman without an escort risked going out at night. What a change occurred when such men as Col. Pringle, Dr. Hollifield, Dr. Whitaker, Col. Evans, Col. Lee Warthen, Messrs. E. A. Sullivan, B. E. Roughton, B. J. Tarbutton, E. H. Mitchell and dozens of others determined to rid not only the town but the county of the disgrace of being a liquor stronghold. By united effort, a new Sandersville was created. Out of evil, sometimes God permits good to result.

Brick Structures. In 1886, by the carelessness of a man throwing down a burning cigarette into a pile of shavings, the east side of the square was burned. The next year fire broke out on the north side, that whole line went down in flames. From the ashes, instead of wooden buildings, brick structures were erected, and a new Sandersville from a business standpoint was born.

Cotton Warehouses. Until 1895, cotton was bought on the streets, there were no warehouses. Now we have two, and before the visit of the boll weevil, we stored many thousands of bales each season, besides the thousands shipped immediately.

Organization of Public School System. Sandersville has always had good schools. Before the war, men and women noted for their culture, as well as education, conducted private schools. Later, after the war, Southern men and women, among them Miss Ella Brookins, Mrs. Keyes, and Miss Mollie Whitehead, began to teach. Thus when the time came, such men as Dr. A. C. C. Thompson, Mr. Ivy W. Duggan, Captain Hugh Lawson, with two gentlemen as assistants, made Sandersville an educational center. 1880 saw the organization of the Public School System. Mr. Harris Brantley, father of Mrs. C. R.

Pringle, gave the school lot to the city. Mr. Brantley and Mr. Pringle, with their servants planted the elms which still shade the campus. The wooden structure was replaced in 1897 by a brick building, now the Grammar School. The chairmen of the committee from the city and from the Board of Education were Messrs. Wiley Harris and W. A. McCarty. In 1910 the High School was erected. 1916 saw the completion of the Vocational Building, Chairmen S. G. Lang and William Hovey Smith. Our school buildings would do credit to a larger town, three large brick structures that aggregate a value of many thousand dollars. Boys and girls from our school who are graduates can enter any college in Georgia without examination. Sandersville owes much to her school and equally as much to her Sanitarium. From a village of 300 fifty years ago, she now numbers 3,000. So much for the past—now for what she is today.

Rawlings' Sanitarium. We own an institution that makes people from large cities wonder, our Sanitarium. It has not only a State reputation, but is widely known all over the South. The celebrated Mayo Brothers of Rochester, Minn., have said that the head of the Institution, Dr. William Rawlings, is one of the best surgeons in America.

A FAMILIAR SCENE OF OLDEN TIMES

CHAPTER VI.

SANDERSVILLE CONTINUED

Industries. Our electric plant and water system are excellent. We have one of the few potato curing houses in the South. Until the death of Mr. Wiley Harris, we had an up-to-date flour mill and steam ginnery. Our cotton seed oil mill gave employment to many and was a success until it was destroyed by fire. Our banks are all first class and each does a fine business. There is not a vacant store or vacant dwelling in town. Goods can be bought cheaper in our stores than in the cities. The hotel and boarding houses are first rate. Stephens Ice & Coal Company makes pure ice and supplies a large territory. We have four planing mills. B. B. Lovett's Red Bird plant which has an output of two million feet per month, ships lumber to foreign countries. The I. B. Lieberman Company ships more than half a million feet a month, much of which is sent to Eastern markets. T. I. Harrison's mill has an output of over half a million, so has the new firm of Beam Lumber Company. This enterprise gives employment to many. Lang's Variety Works was established over thirty years ago. It is the largest of its kind between Savannah and Macon. Everything necessary to building can be found in this establishment. Holt Bros. sale stables and J. D. Newman's sale stables bring fine mules and horses from the West. Shelnutt & Smith's business is one that helps the farmers dispose of their produce.

Churches. We have five churches, all of which have regular services. Sandersville was the first in the county to have a church of the Disciples of Christ (Christian), and the Catholics built a church here in 1870. The Episcopalians had the first brick church in the town. The Methodists and Baptists were here from the early days, and at first used the same edifice.

An incident in the history of the building of the new Methodist church. Some time about the year 1856 four young men, all of whom were dressed in linen clothes as was the fashion in that day, attended services at the old Methodist Church. It was located on the hill in the City Cemetery on the old Milledgeville road. The building was old and dilapidated and the red dust had sifted through the cracks and covered the seats in the church, and when these four young men came out they discovered that their clean linen suits had become much soiled from contact with the red dust. They began the agitation for the building of a new church, each making a cash contribution of $100.00, which was followed by contributions from others until a sufficient amount was raised for the building of the new church. The lot was given by Silas Floyd and the site selected was where the present brick church now stands. The singular thing about this incident is, that none of these four young men were members of the Methodist Church and only one of them became a member of it, the other three became affiliated with the Baptist Church. These young men were B. D. Evans, J. T. Youngblood, Thomas E. Brown, and J. U. Floyd.

The County Officials have offices in the Court House, which was re-built in 1899.

Library. We boasted of a library second to none in the State, until it was destroyed by fire in 1921. With untold energy, its sponsors have again accumulated two thousand volumes.

W. C. T. U. Woman's work is second to none in the Tenth District. The W. C. T. U., organized here in the early days of its existence in the United States, is the pioneer in good works. Its first President, Mrs. B. J. Tarbutton, labored early and late for its success. Year after year different departments of its work were taken up, until now with a membership of over a hundred active members, it does excellent work in every way. Child welfare is the latest department being operated.

The Woman's Club was organized in 1919. Its first President was Mrs. C. D. Shelnutt. Everything required of a federated body it does. The various departments of works are in the hands of efficient committees.

The Mary Ann Williams Chapter, Daughters of Confederacy, was organized in 1897 in Sandersville at the home of Mrs. S. M. Hitchcock. Miss Mary Mildred Gilmore was chosen as first President. Mrs. John Quinn is President at this time.

One of the first services of love and duty undertaken by the chapter was the marking of Confederate graves. Crosses of Honor have been bestowed upon all veterans. One of the pleasant customs for the past twenty-two years has been the serving of dinner on Memorial Day to the veterans and their families, and for the past few years to the World

War Veterans also. The chapter has about one hundred members, making a representative in nearly every home in the city. These are loyal and true and as long as our Southland lives, just as long will there be found willing minds and hearts to teach the "story of the glory" of those who wore the gray.

CONFEDERATE FOUNTAIN MEMORIAL
ERECTED BY THE
J. D. FRANKLIN CHAPTER
UNITED DAUGHTERS OF THE CONFEDERACY
AT TENNILLE, GEORGIA

CHAPTER VII

TENNILLE

From 1837 to 1843, the Central of Georgia Railroad was being built from Savannah to Macon. At that time, numbers instead of names were given to stations, so what is now the thriving city of Tennille was then Number Thirteen C. R. R. At one time it was proposed to call the town that grew adjacent to the station, Franklin, because much of the land in the surrounding district was the property of a wealthy farmer, Sam O. Franklin. However, it was finally named for Benjamine Tennille, who also was an owner of much land.

Railroad Center. Until after the War Between the States, Tennille was but a village. It grew rapidly and is now a wide-a-wake and progressive city, a railroad center, the terminus of the Wrightsville & Tennille, the Georgia & Florida, the Sandersville Railroad, and is an important station on the Central of Georgia.

It is one of the **trade centers** of this section, a fine shipping point for cotton. Much farm produce as well as live stock is brought for market.

Industries. Tennille is lighted by electricity, and possesses water works, the reservoirs being filled by artesian wells. There are planing mills, a cotton oil mill, and two well known wholesale grocery companies. Washington Manufacturing Company has 125 employees. Its chief product is standard army duck, which is dyed many beautiful colors and used for awnings, tents, and other purposes.

The citizens of Tennille take great pride in their homes and their premises, in fact, their **civic pride** is second to none in the State.

The Public School System. Mr. Lawson Kelley donated to the town the land and the wooden building—first school house in Tennille—in 1881. In 1896 a brick building was being constructed by the side of the old one, but before it was completed, both houses burned. In 1897 the present brick building was finished, it is now used for the Grammar School. The High School was built in 1915.

Among the educators of the past, as well as one of the best beloved pastors, is the Rev. T. J. Beck who has been a resident of Tennille for more than thirty years. Others prominent in educational work were W. L. Duggan, W. F. Dykes, and E. W. Marshall. Dr. Ed. Holmes, famed as an educator,

WASHINGTON COUNTY, GA. 43

especially of boys, is a Tennille boy. For years he was at Mercer, then at Barnesville, now President of G. M. C. at Milledgeville.

There are **three churches,** the Baptist, the Methodist, and the Christian.

Tennille felt the full force of **Sherman's march** to the sea, one column of his forces passed through it, destroying everything in its path. It was in Tennille that, by Sherman's orders, the railroad iron rails were heated and twisted so that they would be useless.

Near Tennille, on the old Irwin plantation, in the family graveyard rests the dust of **Governor Jared Irwin.**

Among the **Early Settlers** were Messrs. William Sneed, Lewis Bullard, John Smith, and Sam O. Franklin, all of whom were farmers, large land owners, who understood the institution of slavery and were kind, considerate masters. Except Mr. Franklin, all of them lived adjacent to Tennille. Mr. Franklin owned a beautiful estate in the town. Later came Mr. William Harman who moved near Tennille from Sandersville. He was a merchant and was connected with the Central of Georgia Railroad. His nephews, William N. Harman and Captain John C. Harman, soon after the war became identified with every enterprise in Tennille. Sturdier, more reliable men, truer friends never existed. James Berrien Stephens was one of the most progressive planters the county has produced. He developed special strains of oats, potatoes, and peas which were named for him. He was a true Confederate soldier, enlisting in 1861 at the age of sixteen.

Cultivation of the Peach. In 1868, Captain Ben S. Boatright with William Moultrie Moses began the cultivation of the peach for the market. Their success was phenomenal, their orchard known far and wide. Later, Captain Boatright devoted his entire time to farming, especially to the raising of cotton. He was badly wounded in the war, from the effects of which he never entirely recovered. His last years were spent in Tennille, where he moved his family some years ago.

In the Late Seventies, Messrs. T. N. and J. W. Smith, both of Washington County, near Warthen, opened a mercantile business in Tennille and soon became among its most prosperous citizens. Both of them were well trained business men, good citizens, firm believers in righteousness, strong for that which was upbuilding. They were succeeded in business by their nephews, Messrs. Tom and Joe Rich Smith.

Other men who helped to build up Tennille in days gone by were Messrs. Tom Cook, Seaborn and Lawson Kelly, all men of sterling worth, whose children and grandchildren are among the best people of Tennille and of Washington County.

It is impossible within the scope of this little volume to mention every one who has done something for the development of our section. But mention must be made of the late **Robert Kelley,** so long the head of the Farmer's Union of Washington County. His name was a synonym of progress. Closely associated with him was **Mr. James Kelley,** conceded now to be the foremost farmer of Washington County.

Tennille shares with Sandersville the honor of being the home of Governor **Thomas W. Hardwick.** He spent his childhood, boyhood and young manhood in Tennille, his mature years in Sandersville.

Captain Charles Jacobson, who made himself and his county famous during the World War, was born, reared, and educated in Tennille.

Porter Davis, although reared in the country, received his schooling until he entered college in Tennille. He has represented the United States in France and Siam, and is now on consular duty in China, located at Shanghai.

HISTORY OF

Mayors of Tennille

The first mayor of Tennille was **Captain James D. Franklin,** one of the heroes of Washington County in the war of 1861-1865.

The present mayor of Tennille is **T. W. Smith,** son of Mr. John Smith, who was one of the progressive farmers in the days of Reconstruction.

Captain John C. Harman, prominent as a lawyer and as County School Superintendent, for years postmaster, was very popular when mayor of Tennille.

Clem. Brown for sixteen years served the people loyally as mayor. He was identified with every public interest of the town. For thirty-six years he was one of the most prominent men of the city and had hosts of friends throughout the county. For ten years he was a member of the City Board of Education and served as President several terms.

Herbert Mitchell Franklin was mayor several terms, President of the Farmers and Merchants Bank, State Legislator twice, one of the most enterprising men Washington County has produced. Promoter of the Tennille Ad Club, organizer and developer of the buying and shipping of farm products, identified with every interest for the development of the county, he is noted as one of the foremost men of the times.

Prominent Women

Among the literary women of Tennille is **Mrs. Loula Kendall Rogers,** a poetess and author of great note, beloved by every one. She is the Poet-Laureate for the U. D. C. of Georgia, and has won many prizes and distinctions for her poems and writings. No woman is more loyal to her friends, her country, and her church. It can truly be said that she is one of God's "nobly planned."

Mrs. Herbert M. Franklin, daughter of Mrs. Loula Kendall Rogers, adopted Tennille as her home upon her marriage to Herbert M. Franklin. Few women in the State are more generally admired and beloved than she. Whatever is worthwhile doing, she undertakes. Besides all the local work she has fostered, she is State Historian of the U. D. C., a member of the Board of Visitors of the Georgia State College for Women, Milledgeville, trustee of the Soldiers Home, Atlanta. During the period of the World War, she was State President of the Daughters of the Confederacy. From its organization, she has sponsored the Major General Samuel Elbert Chapter,

D. A. R., and all other clubs for the upbuilding of her town and county. Mrs. Franklin is now chairman of the State D. A. R. Library, as well as State Librarian.

Mrs. C. D. Hardwick is one of Tennille's best known women. She is tireless in her efforts in promoting the welfare of the city. She is the aunt of ex-Governor Thomas W. Hardwick.

Clubs

The Daughters of the Confederacy is the oldest club in Tennille. Soon after its organization in the State, Mrs. George Franklin urged the formation of a chapter. She was the first President. The name chosen was that of Captain James D. Franklin. He built a club house for his namesake, and did much to promote its interests. Among the things the Daughters accomplished was marking the soldiers' graves, presenting an interesting program each Memorial Day, entertaining the veterans, and erecting a fountain in the center of the square.

The Daughters of the American Revolution was organized in 1913. It was named in honor of the Revolutionary hero, Major General Samuel Elbert.

WASHINGTON COUNTY, GA.   49

Its greatest work at present is compiling a Genealogical History of Washington County.

Government Markers have been obtained for the graves of the following soldiers of the Revolution buried in this section:

1. John Jordan, North Carolina, member of Colonel Samuel Elbert's Regiment, buried in the old family burial ground at the Jordan home, which is more than one hundred years old.

2. Moses Newton, South Carolina, member 2nd South Carolina Infantry, brother of Sergeant John Newton, buried in the old burial ground near Fenn's Bridge.

3. Francis Tennille, Lieutenant 2nd Batallion Georgia Troops. Buried in old burial ground, eight miles from Tennille, five from Sandersville.

4. Daniel Shehe, Corporal in Colonel John Patkis Regiment, old burial ground near Davisboro.

5. George Franklin, Baptist preacher in charge of Jordan's Church at Davisboro (now extinct) from 1808 until his death in 1816. He served in Georgia Legislature and was a member of Constitutional Convention in 1788. Land grant in Franklin County for Revolutionary service. Buried in old burial ground near Davisboro. (First of three generations

to serve in Georgia Legislature. His son S. O. Franklin and grandson H. M. Franklin served.)

6. William Franklin, father of George Franklin, founder of one of the earliest Baptist Churches in Georgia, Little Brier Church, generally known as Franklin's Meeting House. He had a grant of land in Washington County for services in the Revolution. He is supposed to be buried in old burial ground near Davisboro. (Grave has not been marked, as location is uncertain, but records verified.)

7. Charles Jackson, First Lieutenant, Captain Hendricks Company, Benton's Regiment, South Carolina, buried on the Joseph Jackson place.

8. William Hunt, Member Colonel William Chandler's Regiment, buried near Davisboro.

9. Colesby Smith, buried near Tennille.

10. Joseph Sessions, Revolutionary Soldier. Buried on Capt. B. S. Boatright's place.

11. Benjamin Sessions, 1812 soldier. Buried on Captain B. S. Boatright's place.

Revolutionary Heroes

All of the men who received grants from the U. S. Government were Revolutionary soldiers. Many are mentioned by White in his statistics, but the D. A. R. Chapters after much research have given other names, among them, William Gainer, B. Tarbutton, John Sparks, William Warthen, William Hood, Alexander Lawson. (List furnished by Tennille Chapter, D. A. R.)

The Woman's Club was organized in 1914. Its first President was Mrs. Buford Smith. The outstanding achievement of the Club is the building of a memorial Club House to honor the soldiers of the World War.

The Fine Arts Club was organized in 1920. Its aim is to cultivate the mind and to make the homes of Tennille more beautiful and attractive.

There are several social clubs, among them the **L. O. P. H.** and **Not-A-Chance.**

The Tennille Ad. Club, composed of the merchants and business men, is one of the livest and most progressive clubs of the city.

CHAPTER VIII.

RIDDLEVILLE

The beginning of this quaint typical Middle Georgia town was due to the generosity of a pioneer, Mr. Anderson Riddle, who came to Georgia in 1815 and settled near the town that bears his name. He was an ardent advocate of education, so when the opportunity came he offered to the Mount Vernon Baptist Association the land, three hundred acres, and money to help build the school, to be called Mount Vernon Institute. The town that built around the Institute was called Riddleville. It was incorporated by an Act of the Legislature in 1859, at the same time Mount Vernon Institute was chartered. One provision of the charter was that no intoxicants could be sold within a radius of three miles of the school, unless by the vote of a majority of the best citizens. Of course the outcome was—no liquor, even in the day when it was sold at every crossroad and frequently several grog shops still nearer together.

The Institute was governed by a board of fifteen men selected by the association. The first chairman was Rev. W. I. Harley of Sparta, the secretary Rev. J. R. Taylor, the first teacher Prof. T. J. Evans. About this time James A. Page gave twenty acres to the school.

Until the outbreak of the War Between the States the school flourished. Then for four years there were but few sessions.

Under Rev. J. J. Hyman, who was Principal for eight years from 1875 to 1883, the school was built up.

In 1891 at a meeting of the association the title of the school property was conveyed to the Baptist Church at Riddleville.

The town grew slowly because remote from the railroad. It was not invaded by Sherman's troops.

Of late years it has developed into an enterprising town; many of our prosperous farmers and business men live within its limits, among which are the Fulghums, Bryans, Pages, Pates and Riddles.

The first mayor and aldermen were members of the Mt. Vernon Association.

Mr. W. H. Fulghum, a veteran of the War Between the States, made Riddleville his home for many years. He was a man who always stood for the right. In sorrow or trouble the community turned to him for consolation or advice.

DAVISBORO

Davisboro is an old town, being third in age, Warthen first, Sandersville next, then Davisboro. It was suggested to call it Hardwick for William Hardwick, great grandfather of ex-Governor Hardwick, but as there was already a town of Hardwick, it was decided to name it for the grandfather of Mr. T. J. Davis. That Mr. Davis had come from North Carolina and bought much land in and near the present town of Davisboro. From the best authority that we can get, it was named about 1827. In 1842 when the Central of Georgia Railroad passed through it, it was called Number 12.

Some of the most prominent men in the county have lived there. Besides the Davises and the Hardwicks—such men as the Harrises, Jordans, Newsomes, Baileys, Thigpens, Cheathams, Gainers and Halls all lived in or near the town.

The town felt the force of the war—was left in ruins by Sherman.

In February of 1883, it was almost destroyed by a cyclone. It was the most terrific storm that had visited the county in the memory of the oldest inhabitants. In a few years it was rebuilt, and is now one of the most thriving towns of this session.

Its artesian water from flowing wells is excellent. It has a fine school system, three churches and several up-to-date stores.

For several years it was the home of Doctors A. L. and D. L. Cheatham. At one time Dr. Julian Evans practiced medicine there.

Elsewhere we have spoken of Messrs. Isaac and Abe Hermann who made it their home before the war of 1861. Among later men of prominence are the Taylors, the Aldreds, the Orrs, the Bealls.

Davisboro was incorporated in 1894 by an Act of the Legislature, the first mayor was A. W. Aldred, his council was N. H. Jordan, J. H. Evans, T. J. Orr, O. H. P. Beall and W. G. Bailey.

The masons have a strong lodge composed of very earnest men.

The women of Davisboro are well organized; they have a Federated Club, W. C. T. U., several Missionary Societies, and two or three social clubs.

OCONEE

Oconee was settled when the Central of Georgia was built, about 1842. It was then called Station Number Fourteen. Some of the finest people of the county have their homes in or near Oconee. In days gone by they were the Snells, Joyners, Woods, McAfees, Graybills, Elkins, Smiths, McBrides and Hodges. Many of the families who now live there bear these honored names.

Oconee was the scene of a battle between the Georgia Cadets and the other State Troops with a Regiment of Federals belonging to Sherman's men.

A few years ago Oconee was struck by a fearful tornado, and much of the town was swept away. The casualties were many; however, the citizens soon rallied and rebuilt.

The Cleveland-Oconee Lumber Company is the biggest industry in Washington County. The president is Mr. Neal Meier. There are three hundred employees. The monthly output is one hundred and fifteen car loads. As a side line the company owns pecan orchards, numerous saw mills and planing mills all over the county.

HARRISON

This town is unique in that it was named for its first mayor, who was also its express agent, railroad agent and postmaster, and a director of the road. It received its name in 1883 when the Wrightsville and Tennille Railroad was built.

Mr. Green B. Harrison, a wealthy farmer, gave the railroad right of way through his property. Mr. Harrison was a native of Washington County. His foreparents were among those who came to Georgia at the close of the Revolution, and had land grants in this county.

The town has some very fine progressive citizens. Before the boll weevil made its inroads, Harrison was quite a cotton market. Its school is well graded, and well taught.

It is the home of such men as Dr. E. S. Peacock, J. M. Whitaker, the McAfees, and News. Besides, the Harrisons, the Woods, Peacocks, Smiths, Brantleys, Youngs, Pages and Joiners have done much to make the town progress.

Among the prominent men who have lived in Harrison are the Rev. James Raiford Wood, A. W. J. Wood, Honorable Wade H. Wood and Dr. John G. Harrison.

DEEPSTEP

Deepstep, on the upper Milledgeville road, is a new town that grew rapidly from a hamlet that was formed by a few property owners building near one of the chartered camp grounds of the county. At one time it was one of the famous camp meeting places for the Methodist people in Washington, Baldwin, and other nearby counties.

In December, 1900, the town was chartered by Act of the Legislature with the following Mayor and Council: Dr. J. E. Peeler, Mayor, Messrs. M. N. O'Quinn, A. S. Avant, L. A. Gladdin, W. A. Walker, and O. F. Veal, Aldermen.

The town has grown rapidly. The inhabitants have a great deal of town pride. It is in the center of a fine agricultural district. Here is located one of the County High Schools, which has ten grades and a fine corps of teachers.

The Baptists and the Methodists have each a church building on the outskirts of the town. There is a mill and a ginnery near the town limits.

CHAPTER IX.

SLAVERY

When the county was first settled there were very few slaves, for most of the settlers were Revolutionary soldiers who came with their families through the wilderness to make homes for themselves. When Virginians, North Carolinians and others from Maryland came, they brought slaves almost without an exception, because from the beginning of the eighteenth century there were many negroes in all the States, except Georgia. Under her Constitution slavery and liquor were forbidden.

After awhile both of those laws were changed. In course of time many negroes were brought into the county. While many persons bought them after the cotton gin was invented, a man who speculated in negroes was not respected by the best class of citizens. Many masters were kind, just as most parents are kind, but there were a few who were cruel, and some bought them in other states to sell them in Georgia. In the greater number of cases, the white people were good to the negroes, and the negroes were good to their owners. This was proved during the War Between the States. While the masters were away, the slaves protected those left at home and worked for them. There was devotion between the white children and their colored playmates. When, as was sometimes the case, the master or young master, fell upon the field of battle, the negroes at home helped to bury them, then worked to help "Mistis" support the family and to care for the young negroes.

As an institution, slavery was not popular in Georgia, but our people fought for State's rights, not for slavery.

SHERMAN'S MARCH THROUGH WASHINGTON COUNTY

Often the impressions made upon a child's mind are deeper and more lasting than upon the mind of an older person.

For months, my little friends and I had heard that the "Yankees" would surely come from Atlanta through our section on their way to the sea.

In November, 1864, day after day reports came that Sherman was "coming through." Finally he did come with fifteen thousand men. He had divided his Sixty Thousand force into four columns

WASHINGTON COUNTY, GA. 61

covering a width of sixty miles from Atlanta to Savannah. We were in his path, as one of the old routes was the old Louisville Road that led directly through Sandersville from Milledgeville to Savannah.

Digressing a bit, for this is of vital interest to us as Southerners and patriots, Mr. Ben R. Smith, uncle of Messrs. Louis, Willis and George Evans, also of Messrs. Lee and Lopez Smith and others owned a beautiful home on the Deepstep Road. It was about four miles from town. Like most Southern homes it was noted for its hospitality; there was always a welcome for the stranger as well as for the friend. Mr. Smith knew that there were home on furlough at least a dozen of the Washington Rifles, so he gave them a sumptuous dinner. Mrs. Smith and her sister, Mrs. Horne, were the hostesses. About the time the guests were seated, one of the house servants named Isham came in hurriedly, he was a very black man, on this occasion, he was ashen with fright. He exclaimed, "Lord, Marse Ben, the woods on the hill are full of blue coats." Mr. Smith answered, "Isham, you black rascal, if you are fooling me, I'll skin you." Isham said, "Marse Ben, come and see." All hurried to the front piazza. Sure enough, three hundred of the blue coated enemy were on the hill.

No one stood on the order of his going. Fortunately their horses stood bridled and saddled. For once, forgetting the ladies and Southern chivalry, they dashed away. Among the fleeing Confederates was Colonel Thomas Wells whose horse was shot, and fell. Of course, Colonel Wells was made a prisoner. One man, named Cofield, in his excitement jumped from his horse, took his saddle, leapt the fence and stood marking time. He too fell into the hands of the enemy. Captain Frank Brantley, who lived near Jordan's Mill escaped. So did several others by rapid riding. Mr. Green Bell, uncle of W. A. Bell, was shot through the thigh, his horse galloped away. As he lay in the fence corner expecting to be killed, Dr. H. N. Hollifield, riding a powerful bay, drew rein and lifted Mr. Bell before him and spurred for liberty, the doctor's cavalry overcoat and hat were riddled by bullets. The advance guard pursued no further than the hill beyond our city limits. Dr. Hollifield took Mr. Bell to his home, comforted his family by attending to the wounded man, then went to his own home to bid his family goodbye, he and the others of the party escaping were trying to join their command beyond the Ogeechee.

While this was occurring, a rumor was circulated, exciting the women and children, that a large band of Yankees were coming up the Tennille Road. My father, who was hopelessly ill from a crushed lung, (father had trained near Savannah with the first troops that went to Virginia, but hemmorrhages prevented his being accepted, the kick of a horse had crushed his ribs into his lung) was up here and could not get conveyance back to Savannah. The Confederacy had commandeered all the means of travel to move government supplies. When mother excitedly told him of the near approach of the supposed Yankees, father went out to the gate, I at his heels. Sure enough the clattering of many galloping hoofs could be heard. I, seated on the gate post, saw the troops coming, but they wore grey. Father calmed the excited neighbors, all women and children by telling them it was a troop of our soldiers. Just then, a small, very erect man, dressed in grey, wearing a crimson sash and a large black plumed hat, drew rein and said, "Friend, is it true that Sherman's cavalry has had a skirmish with a few Confederates about four miles out?" Father saluted and answered, "Yes, General Wheeler, it is true." General Wheeler inquired, "Who told you?" Father said that Dr. Hollifield who was in the party that was surprised by the Federal Cavalry had ridden by and told us. Then General Wheeler spoke to an orderly, asking father to give the man directions to Dr. Hollifield's home. Presently the orderly returned with Dr. Hollifield who accompanied General Wheeler's thousand men to the hill beyond Mr. Smith's.

Later in the evening, a skirmish occurred in which thirteen Federal soldiers were made prisoners. Captain Deason, one of the prisoners, was severely wounded, and was cared for at the home of Brother Anthony at his earnest request. The prisoners were brought into town and a barracks improvised in a store which stood where Harris & West's Drug Store now stands. During the night the sentries placed by General Wheeler's order were overpowered and rendered senseless before they could make an outcry. Upon investigation by court martial demand of President Davis, by General Wheeler, it was found that the fiendish deed was done by some camp followers. The eleven prisoners of war were silently stolen away to a field on the Flournoy Place and shot. This was horrible. All right thinking people condemned it, none more than General Wheeler and his troop. My father, Mr. Bell, who was too badly wounded to go with the other soldiers on furlough, Mr. Pincus Happ, Rev. James Anthony, and Dr.

James R. Smith were the only men left in town. About three o'clock, Mr. Happ came in his carriage for father to go with him to bury the soldiers for the sake of humanity, and because he felt sure that in revenge that if General Sherman did come through town, all the inhabitants would be killed and the town burned. Mother was afraid for father to go, he was so ill, but he went and took the two negro men servants we had up here. Mr. Happ had his men. They buried the dead and returned before day. Father sent his men on to Savannah to their families. They were afraid of the Yankees and departed in a hurry.

General Wheeler had no idea it was one of the main divisions of Sherman's army, so early on Friday evening prepared to camp on the hill in a field, where Captain Isaac Herman's home afterward stood. A plum orchard and pine thicket were between the town and that hill. The men from whom father had hired teams for the negroes and necessary camping outfits and a carriage for us had run themselves and their animals into the swamps, thus leaving us no way to get to our home in Savannah. We were at breakfast, father lying on a couch, mother, brother and I at the table, and the baby in the nurse's arms. We heard firing of rifles and yelling of men, then came a clattering of horses' hoofs, and a rain of bullets on the roof. Wheeler's men went dashing by, firing as they went. The road was a mass of blue men, the surrounding fields were full of them. In a few minutes our house was filled with the surging mass. In a little while there was not a piece of china, silver, or even the table cloth left, and the food disappeared in a second. Fences were torn down, hogs shot, cows butchered, women crying, children screaming, pandemonium reigned. Then the jail, the court house, people's barns and a large factory that made buckets and saddletrees, which stood where the Catholic Church now stands, were all ablaze. At that time, General Sherman found out about the shooting of the twelve prisoners of war, so he ordered the town razed. Then old Brother Anthony, the Methodist preacher, went to him in the name of the women and children, declaring that those who did the atrocious deed were not even Georgians, much less inhabitants of Sandersville and Washington County. The stern commander was not moved. Brother Anthony plead in the name of the Christ, but General Sherman was not a Christian. He did not care if delicate women and little children perished in the cold. Finally, Brother Anthony tried a masonic sign. That had its effect. The town was saved and a guard stationed in every house, after everything of value and of comfort had been destroyed. From Saturday morning until Monday, many inhabitants had neither food nor water. It seems beyond belief that not a chicken was left, not a hog, and only a few cows, no meal nor flour, the ground was strewn with food, carpets were drenched with syrup and then covered with meal. Negro soldiers entered private homes and searched for valuables. My mother refused to unlock her bureau drawers, but a soldier placed his bayonet at her back and forced her to march in front of him. Father was helpless from a terrible hemorrhage brought on by excitement, to save him she obeyed the Yankee's command, then he helped himself to all valuables that she had overlooked when hiding some treasures.

Verily, Sherman made war horrible.

What happened in town was duplicated wherever a plantation was in the line of march. Women had to see servants, arrayed in their mistresses' dresses, depart with the invaders. Young ladies stood helplessly by while their maids rode off on their favorite horses. Even graves in country churchyards were opened. In one instance, a country home was burned, all the furniture with it except a piano. This, one of the faithful slaves begged for, because he could not bear to have his young mistress's "pianner" burned. He took it to his cabin, and as soon as the marauders moved on, he, with the help of other negroes who loved their white folks, hid it in the swamp, and covered it with blankets and quilts. There it stayed for six months until the family returned and rebuilt.

Mont Ariel. Many years ago a Mr. William Skrine owned a beautiful place in Washington County, two miles north of Sandersville. He, because of its being located upon a hill, named it Mont Ariel. The mansion was built, as all Colonial ones were, with a broad colonnade, tall columns supported the roof that extended over the colonnade. The halls were wide, the rooms large, the ceilings high, the staircase was of mahogany. Bookcases were built into the walls, lining the library on three sides. It was a magnificent building. The grounds were naturally attractive, and the owner improved them wonderfully. At Mr. Skrine's death, it was bought by a family from Savannah named Hardee, for a summer home. Then a landscape gardener was employed who adorned the great lawn, already shaded by mighty oaks, with marble urns, and statues. The flower garden was surrounded by a hedge of English Hawthorne, everything that money could do was done to make it an ideal home. Then came the war, with ruin in its train. The place was dismantled by Sherman and then it passed from one owner to another, each time it became less valuable. Finally, the house was destroyed by fire. This place is a type of several that were built in the county "before the war."

This record could be made very long, relating all that did happen, but the incidents told are enough to impress upon the minds of the children the horrors of war.

The young people of the county should be told that the largest number of troops to offer for service from any county came from Washington County.

From a roster compiled by the late Major Mark Newman, I append the following:

Roster of Confederate Soldiers

In 1861, the population, according to the census of the preceding year, numbered 6143 white males and females. Of that number, the males were 1460, from fifteen years to fifty, ages suitable for military duty.

The companies were organized in Washington County and served in Virginia, the West, Georgia, and home defense.

1. Washington Rifles, Capt. S. A. H. Jones, 144 men.

2. Irwin Volunteers, Capt. Tully Graybill, 76.

3. Sandersville Volunteers, Capt. T. J. Warthen, 127.

4. Ohoopee Guards, Captain Johnson, 89.

5. Washington Guards, Capt. Carter, 86. (First military company in the county, organized 1821.)

6. Cold Steel Guards, Capt. Newsome, 84.

7. Jackson Guards, Capt. Collins, 110.

8. Martin's Battery, Capt. Howell, 132.

9. 12th Ga. Batallion, Capt. George Peacock, 126.

10. Ga. Light Artillery, Capt. H. N. Hollifield, 115.

11. Washington County Cavalry, Capt. Thos. E. Brown, 54.

12. Wayne Guards, Capt. Thos. F. Wells, 60.

13. 2nd Ga. State Troops, Co. H., Capt. B. D. Evans, 77.

14. Rudisill Artillery, Capt. J. W. Rudisill, 139.

15. Mount Vernon Rifles, Capt. J. P. Jordan, 83.

This totals 1,502, but possibly some 150 names were repeated, as some companies were merged into others, or when time of service expired were transferred into other regiments. However, this proves that it is evident that no other section can show a better record.

  (Signed)   M. NEWMAN,
              Ordinary.

To these might be added Washington County boys, members of the Georgia Cadets, college boys who were in a military school at Marietta.

CHAPTER X.

SCHOOLS OF THE COUNTY

As I have said before, the academies in the county were chartered by the Legislature and they were usually taught by educated men, but here and there were "old field" schools where only reading, spelling and arithmetic were taught, and often very poorly taught. There was another class of school, however, called "neighborhood school," where wealthy men clubbed together and hired a good teacher for their children. Others preferred tutors or governesses. On the plantations of some of the old residents, up to a few years ago, was to be seen the school-room, a pretty little building in the grove near the house, where the tutor or governess taught the children of the family.

The War Between the States caused most of the schools to be closed. All the male teachers entered the Southern Army, or went back North. In the towns some times a woman would open a primary school, but it was not until after the close of the war that large schools were opened. Then the tuition was high. Everything was very high. Many children could not go to school. In 1871, when Georgians, after ten years, were again in charge of the affairs of State, the Public School System was formed by the Legislature that gave every child a chance, for though the term was short, it was free. From that time up to the present, there is no excuse for any white person in the county not being able to read and write.

On December 26, 1851, the famous Washington County Female Institute was chartered with the following board of trustees: William Smith, Green Brantley, Joseph Bangs, James R. Smith, Augustus A. Cullens, William Hodges, Nathaniel Hanies, Isham Saffold, James S. Hook, three of these failing to serve, in their stead were added, Benjamin Tarbutton, Edward Langmade, Haywood Brookins.

Dr. H. N. Hollifield, a fine physician, who loved children and hated ignorance, offered to serve as County School Superintendent until the system was in running order. He loved the work and for several years did it without pay. He was in charge of the county schools until 1895, when he died. He was very ambitious, wanting Washington County Schools to be second to none. Therefore, the teachers were of a high grade.

Mr. John N. Rogers supplied for Dr. Hollifield during his illness and at the doctor's death was elected to the place. He made an excellent official and built up the educational interests of the county. His motto for children was: "Learn by doing." After several terms, Mr. Rogers resigned to do State work.

Mr. Wade Wood of Harrison succeeded him, working hard for the interest of the schools. His successor was Captain John Harman of Tennille who was determined to carry out the principles of his predecessors. Mr. David W. Harrison followed. Early and late he worked to develop the schools, demanding thoroughness of work on the part of the teachers. The present incumbent is Mr. Thomas J. Davis, a man who taught in the county for more than a quarter of a century and therefore knows its needs.

Great Teachers of the Past

Among the great teachers who were here before 1860, were John W. Rudisill, then Dr. A. C. C. Thompson, Captain P. R. Taliaferro, Augustus Bell of Burke, T. J. Cumming, Ivy W. Duggan. These all taught in Sandersville, some of them in other sections of the county.

I have no information as to when Mr. Rudisill came to the county, but I do know he taught a large school in an old wooden building down near what the children called "The Big Gully."

Dr. Thompson was from Maryland. He first taught here in the fifties, then went to the war. After the war he had a select school where boys and girls were thoroughly prepared for college. It was called "A Finishing School."

Mr. P. R. Taliaferro came to Georgia from Virginia in 1858. He was persuaded to open a school for girls only, so he bought the lot where the Christian Church now stands. A wealthy man, familiarly known as "Uncle Billie Smith" erected the school building and set out the water oaks that grew to be the delight of all who passed, so magnificent and shapely were they. When war was declared in 1861, the school was closed, because Captain Taliaferro was among the first volunteers.

Rev. T. J. Cumming taught for many years. For several terms he was a teacher in the Baptist Institute at Linton. Associated with him were such men as Rev. T. J. Adams, and Mr. Ivy W. Duggan. Mr. Cumming spent many years in the school room. There are hundreds of men and women of the older generation who were taught by him in the County Schools. He was Superintendent of the Sandersville Academy in the early years after the war. He gave up the school room to devote his entire time to the ministry.

Mr. Ivy W. Duggan was a teacher before he had reached his majority. He was descended from Irish ancestry. His grandfather came to Washington County from North Carolina soon after the county was laid off. Mr. Duggan's father was a farmer and lived near Warthen. His mother was Miss Elizabeth Walker, of the Walker family, whose grandfather received grants of land because of service in the Revolution. He too settled near Warthen. Mr. Ivy Duggan's education was obtained by a fixed determination that knew no obstacles. With only academic schooling he pushed forward to the goal he had fixed for himself, and received, because of merit, degrees from colleges. He had A. B., A. M., and L. C. D. conferred upon him. He taught at Bethlehem Academy in Washington County, Washington Institute in Hancock in 1860-61, again after the war in 1866-72, Sandersville High School 1873-80, Shorter College 1891-97, Anniston, Alabama College 1898-1907, Tenth District Agricultural School 1907-09. For more than fifty years he was actively engaged in teaching. Faithfulness and duty were passions with him. He led instead of driving, wherever he taught, his pupils loved and reverenced him.

He entered the war in 1861 and was in the service when the war closed.

He was a man of high ideals, a Christian gentleman. Dr. Duggan died September 6, 1917. He had two sons to grow to manhood, Mell L. Duggan, now State Supervisor of Schools, Dr. James R. Duggan who died while Professor of Chemistry at Wake Forest College, North Carolina.

Mr. Hugh Lawson was a descendant of the Hugh Lawson of Revolutionary fame who came to Washington County at the close of the war, having received a land grant for heroism in service. Mr. Lawson served the entire duration of the war 1861-65. At its close, like many young men of that day, he did not know where to turn to make of life a success. Finally, he was prevailed upon to teach. In 1872 he with Mr. W. A. Thomas of Wilkerson County opened a school in Sandersville. This proved just what was needed. At the close of the year, however, Mr. Thomas moved away and Mr. Lawson with Mr. Ivy W. Duggan taught the school with several assistants. It grew in importance until several departments were added to it. In 1880 Mr. Duggan went into college work and Mr. Lawson became Superintendent of the City Public Schools. This position was held by him until 1887 when he resigned to attend to his large farming interests.

No man ever taught that was more popular than Mr. Hugh Lawson. One has said concerning him that he was the largest little man that ever lived. "Nothing mean or low ever came near his head or heart," was said of William Pitt and might well be said concerning Mr. Hugh Lawson—a Southern gentleman of the old type, a Christian ever standing for the right, calm and unafraid.

Reverend J. J. Hyman came of sturdy English stock. His great grandparents settled in North Carolina before the Revolution. His grandparents settled in Warren County. He began teaching in Washington County directly after the War of the Sixties. He was Chaplain of the 49th Georgia Regiment. During his service in the war, his influence over young lives was so strong that he converted and baptized more than two hundred soldiers. At the close of the war, he became Principal of Mount Vernon Institute, Riddleville. He taught in different places. In all, his record as a teacher extends over twenty years. One of the great principles of his life was total abstinence, another was promptness. In the bitter fight between the wets and drys of Washington County, 1878-1886, Mr. J. J. Hyman was a leader, a power. He was a statesman, as well as a teacher and a preacher.

Mr. Augustus Bell (father of W. A. Bell) came from Burke County to be associated with Captain Taliaferro in the young ladies' academy. He was highly educated, courteous, and a Christian. He was very popular with his patrons and with his pupils. He married Miss Lou Tarbutton, a sister of the late B. J. Tarbutton. In 1861 he went to the front to aid in protecting his beloved State from the aggressors' invasion.

CHAPTER XI.

NEWSPAPERS

Washington County's first newspaper was the Telescope published in Sandersville. The year of its beginning cannot be authentically stated, but it can be proven by the files of the Central Georgian that it was well established as early as 1846. Then it was edited by A. G. Ware; a few years afterward the paper was bought by S. Bennett Crafton and its name changed to the Central Georgian. In the early fifties, P. C. Pendleton purchased it and associated with himself, Owen C. Pope, Sr. Then it was simultaneously issued at Sandersville, Sparta and Eatonton, and was at one time the official organ for the notices of the Sheriffs and Ordinaries of Johnson, Emanuel, Laurens, and Montgomery Counties.

In 1855, Sandersville was destroyed by fire, the office of the Central Georgian was consumed, so the printing was done in a house on the premises of P. C. Pendleton who lived where Mr. Horace Mathis now lives.

The Masonic Hall having been burnt, it was rebuilt in 1857, and the lower story occupied by the newspaper plant. At this time, J. M. G. Medlock became part owner. In 1858, Owen Pope moving to Texas, Mr. Medlock became sole owner. In 1866, Col. John N. Gilmore bought it. In 1872 Medlock and Arline became owners of a newspaper, The Sandersville Herald. In 1873, Judge R. L. Rogers joined the corporation as part owner and editor. This arrangement lasted one year, then it was sold to Messrs. John W. Robison, Alex. Robison and W. H. Wylly. Later, Major Joseph Bangs, noted for his deep learning and his keen wit, was editor.

After some years, Messrs. B. D. Evans, Sr., and I. L. Smith owned the paper, with Col. Thomas Evans, editor. Finally it was purchased by Rev. William Park, who was its editor until his death, then the appurtenances of the office were sold to C. B. Chapman of the Progress.

The Mercury, a bright little sheet, was owned and edited by Dr. H. N. Hollifield and Mack Jernigan. It suspended publication about 1881, when Bradford E. Roughton formed a stock company to begin on more pretentious lines. The editors the first year were C. H. Mitchell and Col. S. G. Jordan. Its name was suggested by Editor Mitchell, "The Middle Georgia Progress." Its motto was, "Hew to the line, let the chips fall where they will." From its very inception, the paper was noted for its fearlessness and its fine editorials. At the end of the first year, Col. Jordan resigned, as his legal practice required all of his time. For the following five years, C. H. Mitchell ran it successfully. Mr. Mitchell moved away, then the paper passed from editor to editor, declining in popularity. Finally, it was bought by Mr. C. B. Chapman, and under his management, it is one of the very best weeklies in the South.

COURTS

On May 22, 1787, Hon. Henry Osborne presiding, the first session of the Superior Court was held near Warthen. The following pioneer citizens constituted the first Grand Jury of Washington County: Alexander Irwin, foreman, Elisha Williams, William Johnson, Philemon Franklin, John Robertson, Sr., John Burney, John Martin, James Thomas, Benjamin Tennille, Joshua Williams, Samuel Sinquefield, Joseph Avant, William Irwin, William Shields, John Shafford, John Rutherford, Jacob Dennard, Joseph Beddingfield, Aaron Sinquefield, John Daniel, Sr.

The first Supreme Court Reporter, James M. Kelley, was born in Washington County.

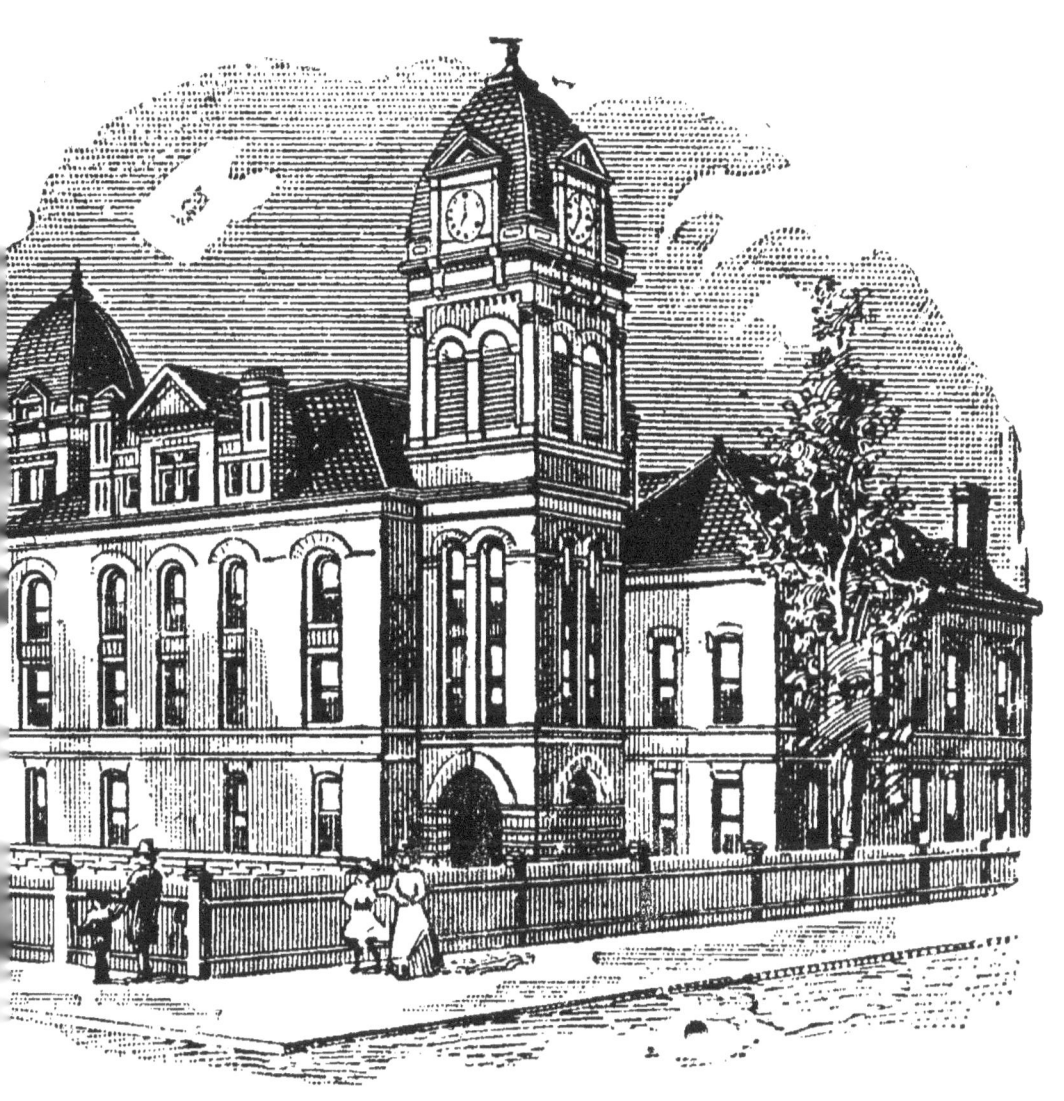

WASHINGTON COUNTY COURT HOUSE

The courts of Washington County are: The Superior Court, the City Court, these are State institutions; Ordinary's Court, Commissioner's Court, Justice Court, County institutions; then Mayor's Court belonging to a town.

There are twenty districts in the county. Two in our county are prescribed by the State. As soon as a section of a county has enough inhabitants to afford one hundred men able to bear arms, it is divided off into a militia district.

The court house officials are: Sheriff, Judge of City Court, Clerk of Superior Court, Ordinary, Tax Collector, Tax Receiver, County School Superintendent, County Commissioners, Court Stenographer. They are always ready to carry out the law. They need the support of the people.

The financial business of the county was formerly handled by the County Treasurer. Since that office has been abrogated, the Commission of Roads and Revenues performs that duty.

Our County has always been fortunate in having the highest type of men for Sheriff. Notable ones were Reuben Mayo, William R. Thigpen, Charles Wall, George Doolittle, and W. M. English, father of the present incumbent. All of these men had ancestors identified with the building up of the county.

ORDINARY

Before the abolition of the Inferior Court, the Judges of that Institution performed the duties of Ordinary. The first Ordinary elected was Major Heyward Brookins, who held the position continuously until his death, in 1875, a period of 23 years. He served during the troublous times of the War Between the States, and the even more trying days of the Reconstruction period. He saved a portion of the records of the county when Sherman raided the town. The major was sick at the time. He sent an official to the Court House for the books, and had them put between the mattresses on the bed on which he lay, thus protecting them.

Upon Major Brookins' death, Judge Clem C. Brown came into office, then Major Mark Newman was elected and served twenty-two years. When he died, Judge Charles C. Thigpen was elected and was in office eighteen years. At his demise in February, 1923, Hon. Thomas Jefferson Swint, who is the incumbent, was inducted into office.

BANKS

The banking system of Washington County was inaugurated by Mr. Louis Cohen in 1885. It was the first one established between Macon and Savannah. Among its first cashiers was Mr. Hermann Bashinsky.

As early as 1871, Mr. George D. Warthen bought out the large merchandise business of Dr. Elisha Parsons of Savannah who had opened his store at the close of the War Between the States. Mr. Warthen began at once to take money on deposit as well as to lend funds. However, his was in connection with his store, not a separate institution until about 1888. For a long time this was the only bank in Washington County, then Tennille opened one, afterwards Davisboro, Harrison, Warthen all had them.

In 1901 the First National Bank was opened in Sandersville with S. M. Hitchcock, cashier. In 1905, the Citizens Bank was formed in Sandersville. Its first cashier was the late James E. Johnson who had his training with George D. Warthen.

The Farmers & Merchants Bank at Tennille was organized 1894. Its first cashier was A. J. McCrary. The Tennille Banking Company opened in 1900 with Julius Bashinski as its first cashier. The Peoples Exchange Bank was organized in 1909. Mr. Julius Bashinski was also the first cashier of this bank.

The Harrison Bank at Harrison (now Holt Banking Company) was established in 1906. Its first cashier was Mr. J. N. Lanier.

The Farmers & Merchants Bank was established at Warthen in 1911. Mr. W. T. Hudgins was the first cashier.

The Planters State Bank was established at Davisboro in 1911. Mr. W. M. Warren was its first cashier.

The Merchants & Farmers Bank was organized at Davisboro in 1908. Mr. S. J. Taylor, Jr., was its first cashier.

CHAPTER XII

FORTS

Two forts were built by the early settlers as defenses against the Indians, one four and one-half miles to the west, the other eight miles south of Sandersville. This one was built by Governor Jared Irwin and his brothers for protection against the war-like Creeks. The remains of the fort are still in existence.

A block house stood for years near Fenn's Bridge on the Jefferson County side. This was built by the great-grandfather of Governor Hardwick for a refuge in case of Indian uprisings.

WAR RECORDS

Washington County has at different times furnished soldiers for six wars: Revolutionary War of 1775, War of 1812, War with Mexico 1846, War Between the States 1861, Spanish-American War 1898, World War 1917.

Many of the old records were burned by Sherman, but the D. A. R. Chapter at Tennille found one grave marked 1812.

Dr. Asa Beach was in two wars, 1846 and 1861. His widow still survives and receives a pension for his services in the Mexican War.

The roster of 1861 shows that Washington County sent more soldiers to the front than any other county of Georgia.

SPANISH-AMERICAN WAR

There were twenty-eight soldiers in the Spanish-American War 1898. However, several others from our county enrolled from other places. Only one of our boys saw service in Cuba, Forrest English of Sandersville, because he had been transferred to the Third Georgia Regiment.

WORLD WAR

In the World War, we again furnished more than our quota. Of drafted men we sent 909, besides there were several hundred volunteers. There were 63 stars on the Sandersville school flag of volunteers, who had at different times been pupils there.

Lieutenant Beverly D. Evans III, was born and spent his boyhood in Sandersville, therefore Washington County claims him. He made the great sacrifice giving up his young life for the freedom of the world. His body lies in the City Cemetery in Sandersville.

Sidney Brown died in Paris after the war from the effects of being gassed. He is buried in the City Cemetery in Sandersville.

Lieut. (Chaplain) Wilbur S. Sewell volunteered November, 1917, from Tennille and was killed in action July 15, 1918.

CHAPTER XIII.

INDUSTRIES AND ITEMS OF INTEREST

The first gin in Washington County was bought by a Mr. Thomas Sparks, grandfather of the late Thomas H. Sparks. It was put up on the Sparks place near Warthen in 1795. The first of the family to move to Washington County came from South Carolina. He received a grant of land for service rendered in the Revolution. The family possess deeds to the land dated 1786.

The old homestead erected in 1793 still stands. On this plantation was grown flax and hemp, but when raising cotton became popular, the other fibrous plants ceased to be cultivated as cotton took much less time to raise, spin, and weave into cloth.

The first department store in the county was that of Quinn Bros., Joe Quinn and his brother, John A. Quinn (father of John H. Quinn). They were from Milledgeville, and operated a store in Sandersville. Later John A. Quinn opened a large department store in Tennille.

If roads are an indication of the intelligence and progressive energy of the public spirit of the county, then our county is coming to the front, because the Dixie Highway through Washington is said to be one of the best stretches in the road.

The tanning of leather was quite an industry in other days. In several sections of the county were tanyards, one of which was located west of Lang's Variety Works. The vats for tanning were there for years after they had been in disuse. The branch that flowed through the land was called Tan Yard Branch.

One of the show places of the county was built by Col. Flournoy. It was for many years known as the Flournoy Place. The plantation was originally owned by the Cullens family, only one of whom still lives, Mr. Ben Rawlings. His brother, Mr. Fred Rawlings, was the father of Dr. William Rawlings, C. G. Rawlings, and Judge B. T. Rawlings. Mr. Ezekial Rawlings was the grandfather of Messrs. A. A. Rawlings, C. W. and George Rawlings. The original Rawlings home was two miles beyond the Flournoy Place, and was approached by going down a long avenue of cedars.

Washington County has the No Fence Law, which has proved very satisfactory.

It has R. F. D. of mails.

It was one of the first counties to adopt the White Primary.

Washington County has the Local School Tax Law.

Among the fraternal organizations are the Masons, W. O. W. and the Kiwanis.

The present population of the county is about 30,000.

Washington county now has the Australian Ballot System.

The Holmes Canning Company, located half way between Tennille and Sandersville, is operated by Edward A. Holmes. The power used is electricity. The processes used are those issued by the Government bulletins. Fully ripe fruit and vegetables that cannot be shipped to market is used, thus saving what would otherwise be wasted. The cannery ships to many points as well as supplies the home market.

There are several poultry farms in the county.

The butchers in the county supply excellent beef and pork to their patrons. Very little Western beef is now shipped into the county.

The sweet potato curing house of Sandersville has induced the planting of the very best sorts of potatoes.

From 1871 to 1877, Washington County held Agricultural fairs on the hill west of Sandersville. This is still called Fair Ground and is a residential section for negroes. Instead of carnivals, horse racing and displays of new inventions were the outside attractions. For several years, young men who rode well held tournaments as the Knights did in days of old. The successful Knight had the privilege of crowning the girl he chose as Queen of Love and Beauty.

Washington County has re-established the annual County Fair. We have one of the best in the State. The industrial exhibit is unequalled, the agricultural exhibit is excellent and always attractively arranged, while the women's work is unparalleled. Then we have live stock and poultry. Many of the exhibits are taken to the State Fair where frequently prizes are won.

Col. T. J. Warthen introduced the steam stationary engine into the county, erecting a saw and grist mill three miles south of Sandersville. In the early days of cotton raising in the county when there were less than half a dozen stores in Sandersville, the merchants placed the cotton bought in front of their stores. Here on moonlight nights, little boys and girls would play, often jumping from bale to bale.

Among the names of the children given us are those of the Ainsworths, Warthens, Renfroes and Smiths.

An old citizen of the county tells this. When the county wished to erect a new Court House, the officials sold the building previously occupied to a man in the country who wished to use it without taking it to pieces, so an endeavor was made to move it. He succeeded by means of blocks, jacks, tackles and mules to get it started, but got no further than where Lang's Variety Works now stands. He abandoned the task, and right in the middle of the road was that big house. It stayed there for six months, people driving around it until the county officials had it torn down.

Washington County has more timber ready to be cut than any county in the section. It leads in both hard woods and pine. There are more than a hundred saw mills in the county, four planing mills in Sandersville, one in Warthen, two in Davisboro, one in Tennille, one at Oconee.

Washington County is second to none in the shipment of cattle. Forty carloads have been shipped in six months. The hog sales are enormous. Chickens are sold by carload lots. Women's Clubs furnish eggs which supply the city trade as well as the

FERN CREST DAIRY

HOOK'S DAIRY, NEAR WARTHEN

home markets. Savannah and Atlanta use cream from Washington County Dairies. The best of cheese has been made at Fern Crest Guernsey Farm.

Fern Crest Dairy with its herd of registered Guernseys ranks first of any in Georgia both in the quality and the quantity of milk produced and the fine strain of cattle. The circular barn where the cows are housed is the admiration of all who visit the place. Dr. William Rawlings, the owner has taken State prizes on some of his herd in fairs of Georgia, and in those of several other Southern states. Fern Crest is the largest and one of the best dairies in the South.

J. H. Hook's Dairy, out from Warthen, is a model one. He owns the largest, finest herd of Jerseys in Middle Georgia. Besides his dairy, Mr. Hooks possesses a flock of Southdown sheep, from the wool of which beautiful blankets have been woven. Mr. Hooks has had suits of clothes made from the wool that were the admiration of those who saw them. Both of these dairies raise everything on the farms attached to supply every bit of feed needed.

Champion's Dairy has a fine herd of registered Jerseys. All the output of this dairy is sold to local trade. Mr. Champion has an up-to-date equipment for handling the milk and for housing his herd.

There are several smaller dairies in the county, proving that this section is awakened to the value of good milk, cream and butter.

Two notable farms in our county are Log Cabin Farm and Fair View Farm. The former, owned by Dr. O. L. Rogers and managed by Mr. J. L. Hall, is famous for its fine breed of hogs, besides for a diversity of crops.

Fair View Farm, owned and operated by Mr. Ben R. Tanner, is considered a model for diversity of crops. Since the arrival of the boll weevil, Mr. Tanner plants everything but cotton. His pecans are flourishing and his young nursery of pecan trees is attractive. He too raises registered pigs.

Mr. Jeff A. Irwin has one of the largest pecan nurseries in the South. His budded trees are always in demand. He can get a market for his nuts where others fail because his are up to the required standard.

Rumph's Nursery, in the southern part of the county, raises fruit, nuts and ornamental trees, as well as flowers of many sorts. The prices are moderate, the plants offered are as fine as those of larger nurseries.

Every sort of food crop that can be raised in the southern part of the temperate zones can be produced here. The farmer of Washington County is not dependent on cotton. Every kind of fruit except tropical fruit can be raised here.

Washington was one of the first counties in the State to ship peaches. B. S. Boatright and W. M. Moses had fine orchards below Tennille, fifty years ago.

The Climate is Fine, Best in the World. Yearly average temperature is about 72 degrees. The annual rainfall is about 48 inches. Epidemics rarely occur.

CHAPTER XIV.

DENTISTS

In this advanced age it is difficult to realize there ever was a time when dentists were unknown within the limits of our county. The doctor who attended one in illness was also the one who "pulled" teeth when they ached. Artificial teeth which looked natural could not be obtained outside of the large cities. In our county the first dentist was Dr. Wilson L. Hollifield, Surgeon Dentist, the first graduate of Dental College, Baltimore. He was a Marylander and came South in 1846. He settled in Sandersville, building a home that stood on the site of the present home of his son, Dr. H. N. Hollifield. It is now owned by the Quinns. His family joined him in 1848. He traveled all over the county, wherever his services were needed. In 1858 Dr. G. W. H. Whitaker came from Philadelphia. He became the junior partner of Dr. Hollifield, with offices on the square.

When the war began in 1861, Dr. Whitaker joined the first company that went from Washington County. Dr. Wilson Hollifield practiced until his death in 1867. Dr. Whitaker was captured in 1864, and remained in prison until 1865. When he returned, he found that Sherman's soldiers had destroyed many of his instruments. It was 1869 before any could be bought. From then until his death in 1890 he practiced. A Dr. Cooley came next, then Dr. Daniel and Dr. Cason. About that time, Dr. Hyman began practicing in Tennille, later Dr. McDade in Tennille and Dr. E. L. Holmes in Sandersville. Several others have opened offices, but remained only a short time. Now Tennille has several good dentists and Sandersville has three, Dr. E. L. Holmes, Dr. H. H. Holliman and Dr. D. Stone.

MISSIONARIES

Washington County has sent to foreign fields as missionaries Misses Clara and Willie Park, the former to China, the latter to Japan.

Mrs. Annie McClendon was sent to Mexico as missionary by the M. E. Church.

Miss Attie Thomas went from the Sandersville High School to do mission work in Laredo.

Miss Laura Mitchell, missionary to China, was born in Sandersville and spent her childhood in her home town.

Mr. Milton Clark of Washington County was for

years a missionary to the Indians in Indian Territory.

Miss Gertrude Avant spent several years as missionary in Indian Territory.

Rev. Owen C. Pope, D. D., was the first Protestant missionary to Mexico. He graduated at Mercer University at the age of eighteen, was ordained the same year and became pastor of several churches. He served in the Confederate army, enlisting in the First Florida Cavalry May 10, 1862. He was pastor of Calvary Baptist Church in New York City, and was sent from there to Mexico as a missionary. Returning to N. Y., he toured the world and on his return he lectured in many cities, using stereoptican views. He founded Simmons University at Abilene, Texas, became its first president, and received his D. D. there. At special request of pupils and patrons, his remains were interred on the campus there.

Ohoopee Church is one of the oldest in the county. It was consecrated in 1792. There were ten men who founded it, among the names are the Daniels, Johnsons, Sheppards, Joiners, Sessions, Burnetts, Orrs, Everetts and Elkins. The original name of the church was Brier Patch. Sherman's horde mutilated the church building and destroyed the records.

CHAPTER XV.

Governor Jared Irwin. Among the first to avail themselves of the opportunity to receive grants of land in the new county of Washington in 1784 were four brothers from North Carolina, Jared, William, Alexander and John Lawson Irwin.

Their grants were in the oak lands on the central part of the original county, now the southern portion of the present county. The descendants of the brothers are still in this section. John Lawson Irwin's grandchildren, Mrs. J. S. Wood of Savannah, Dr. Andrew, Mr. Jeff A. and T. J. Irwin recently erected marking stones in the old cemetery at Irwin's Cross Roads over the graves of the Governor and his brothers.

Governor Irwin was twice elected Governor of Georgia, his first term from 1796 to 1798, his second from 1807 to 1809. The first act of his in 1796 was to sign the rescinding act nullifying the Yazoo Act.

Governor Irwin's mansion in Milledgeville was a log cabin. It stood for many years after Milledgeville became a city.

Jared Irwin, besides being Governor held many positions of trust. He was a Brigadier General of Militia during the Revolution, a member of various Conventions for revising the Constitution of Georgia. From 1790 to 1818 at various times, he was President of the State Senate. He died at his country home in his sixty-eighth year and is buried in the family burial ground.

The only monument erected by an order of the State of Georgia was passed by the Legislature of 1859. It was placed on the court house square in Sandersville and dedicated to Governor Jared Irwin.

Governor Hardwick. After an interval of more than a hundred years, Washington County again furnished a Governor of Georgia. The ancestors of Thomas W. Hardwick moved in 1790 to what was then Washington, now Jefferson County. William P. Hardwick was the first of the name to come to Washington County. He built a block house on the Jefferson side of the river as a defense against the Indians. It had loop holes in it through which Mr. Hardwick and his dependents could fire at the marauders. Later, he moved to what is now Davisboro. He was a planter and a country merchant, owning the largest, at that time, landed estate in this section. The town was called Hardwick.

W. P. Hardwick, great grandfather of the Governor, had one son, Thomas W. Hardwick. He had an only son, Robert W. Hardwick who married Miss Zemula Schley Matthews. They were the parents of Governor Thomas W. Hardwick. His lineage on both sides is in direct descent from men and women famous in the annals of Georgia. Though born in Thomas County, Davisboro became his home when he was three weeks old. After his father's death, his mother moved to Tennille, accompanied by her two little sons, Thomas W. and Walter. The latter died in boyhood.

Governor Hardwick is a great lawyer and statesman. He served in the State Legislature, was a Congressman and a United States Senator. His term as Governor having expired, he has retired to private life and is devoting himself to the practice of his profession.

CHAPTER XVI

PROMINENT MEN

Dr. William Rawlings. Among the great surgeons of the United States is Dr. William Rawlings, a man born and reared on a farm four miles from Sandersville. Both of his great-grandfathers came to Washington County because of land grants they received for service in the Revolution. The Tarbuttons are mentioned in the first group of settlers, the Rawlings only a few years later.

Dr. Rawlings completed his academic course under Dr. A. C. C. Thompson. Then he graduated from Emory College, Oxford. He graduated in medicine first at Baltimore, next at Jefferson College, Philadelphia, then at the University of New York. He began the practice of medicine in Sandersville. After two years successful work, he went to Germany in order to perfect himself in certain intricacies of his profession. Upon his return he again located in Sandersville. In the spring of 1879 he was married to Miss Clara Hollifield, daughter of Dr. H. N. Hollifield. She died in less than a year. After her death he became absorbed in his profession. Physically and mentally very strong, he was tireless, going day and night without apparent fatigue. His recreation was a visit to great specialists to see what there was new in the United States or Canada that he might use. Several times he has made trips to Europe to find some new thing in the medical world. From our section he was the first physician to discover there was more to be learned in some departments of the profession in the Middle West than in the East, hence his visits to Mayo Bros. in Rochester, Minnesota.

Some years ago he became dissatisfied with the old methods of performing operations in the office or in private homes, so he conceived the idea of a sanitarium in Sandersville. He first bought the old hotel, a building that had been erected before the war of 1861. This structure he improved, remodeled, and added to, making at that time a very up-to-date sani tarium. He began with but two nurses, Miss Alice Moses of Columbus, and Miss Mae McKenzie of Nova Scotia, both graduates of New York hospitals. Dr. D. L. Cheatham was after a time associated with him. The demand for a larger building, more nurses, and a corps of physicians became imperative. Then the entire Hotel Julida block was purchased by Dr. Rawlings. It had been previously converted into a sanitarium by Doctors Julian Evans and Henry Hermann. When they dissolved partnership, Dr. Rawlings purchased it from the owners, Tucker & Shelnutt. Today it ranks second to none in the South, with every modern requirement, and its force of physicians, Doctors O. L. Rogers, Fred B. Rawlings, T. B. King, N. Overby, and Miss Mae Jones, with her associate nurses, besides twenty-two nurses in training. About eighteen years ago Dr. Rawlings added a Nurses Training School to his Sanitarium. Every year from five to fifteen young ladies are graduated from the institution.

Like all truly great men, Dr. Rawlings has not been spoiled by success. Quiet, unassuming, gentle in manner, he goes the even tenor of his way, relieving suffering, apparently unconscious of his wonderful knowledge. He has never entered deeply into politics, although he did represent his county in the State Legislature, and the Twentieth Senatorial District (Washington, Baldwin, and Hancock Counties) in the State Senate.

Judge James K. Hines is claimed by Washington County because when a little child, his parents, Mr.

and Mrs. Joseph Hines moved from Burke County to a plantation here. The tract of land included the mill now known as Jordan's Mill, but to us, of an older generation, Hines' Mill.

Out there in the atmosphere of a cultured Christian home, the future judge was reared. He was the only son, his sisters were Misses Susie and Mamie Hines, the former became the wife of Col. S. G. Jordan, the latter is the wife of Judge William Fish of the Supreme Court of Georgia.

Mr. Joseph Hines was a man of sterling worth, of great force of character, a Christian gentleman of the Old South. He believed in church attendance. Every Sunday morning, his carriage driven by a black coachman, beside whom sat an out-rider, whose duty it was to lower the steps of the carriage, approached the steps of the Methodist Church. From the carriage alighted the entire family. They had a special seat near the front.

When Sherman left the people of Sandersville without a particle of food, Mr. Hines sent a wagon load of meat, meal and flour to be distributed among the inhabitants. Fortunately Sherman did not find the Hines plantation or mill.

Reared by such parents, James K. Hines had the best of home influences. He tells this on himself:

"I was going to school in Sandersville, and like most boys, wanted to quit when fishing and hunting were good. I was told I could come home and stay. Of course I had visions of doing nothing but hunt and fish, but the first morning my father called me when the hands went to work. I was to work! My hopes fell. At the end of the week, I was ready to return to school, but my father said, no, I had to work the remainder of the term. It was a lesson I needed."

Judge James K. Hines, when he practiced law, was considered without a peer as a criminal lawyer. Now he is on the Supreme Bench of the State.

Dr. D. Louis Cheatham, though born in Jefferson County, spent his best years in Washington, for on his graduation from the Medical College in Baltimore, he came to Davisboro to be associated with his brother, Dr. A. T. Cheatham. After several years in Davisboro and Atlanta, he moved to Sandersville where he died January 25, 1909. Dr. O. L. Rogers, for several years his partner, said of him: "Dr. Cheatham was a golden-hearted gentleman, true to every trust, steadfast to every duty, sincere to his friends, outspoken on all occasions, a quickness to forgive, a big, grand man, possessing a broad intellect and being a keen observer. He was an extraordinarily fine physician having few equals anywhere.''

He was Mayor of Sandersville for six years. During his administration, he and his council installed electric lights and water. Before the close of his last term, a fine sewerage system was put in. As an official he was ever on the side which his uncompromising ideals pointed out as right. He was perfectly fearless in the discharge of duty, being sincere and true in all of his dealings with all classes of people.

Dr. Cheatham was a direct descendant of one of the Governors of Georgia, Governor David Emanuel of Revolutionary fame being his great grandfather. Like the Governor, Dr. Cheatham was ever true to his convictions, brave, rugged, honest and kind, in sickness and sorrow as gentle and sympathetic as a woman, yet he had strong convictions and the manhood to stand by them.

Oscar H. Rogers. Of all the self-made men of our county, there is no one who deserves honorable mention more than Col. Oscar H. Rogers, father of Dr. Leslie Rogers. From the Memorial Meeting of the Bar in March, 1871, the following facts are gathered. Oscar H. Rogers was no ordinary man. He was the eldest son of Jared Rogers and Elizabeth Williams, both parents of Revolutionary stock. Thus by heredity he was fortunate. His struggle for an education was marvelous. Born in 1851, his school days were between the years 1860 to 1869, just a few months at the time. From 1870 to 1876 he worked for wages on different farms. He was a reader. He made it a daily habit to learn something worth while from books.

In 1877 he was appointed Deputy Sheriff under W. R. Thigpen, Sheriff. Although married, with a family to support, he studied law and was admitted to the bar in 1879. He was successively County Treasurer, serving four years, Mayor of Sandersville, Solicitor General of the Middle Circuit four years, re-elected for another term of four years and died while in office. In June, 1891, after a brief illness, he died in the full vigor of his manhood. He had great common sense, and was a keen observer. He never seemed to have reached the zenith of his mental powers. The rule of his life seemed to be: "To thine own self be true, and it must follow as the night the day, thou canst not then be false to any man." He was in the highest sense a Christian.

Rev. James D. Anthony (father of Rev. Bascom Anthony, so well known in Georgia), was familiarly called by all of us "Brother Anthony." He was a big man, physically, mentally, morally, spiritually. Sermons he preached in my childhood still linger in my memory. Brother Anthony was everybody's friend and preacher, regardless of creed during the war, for he was the counselor of the town and of much of the county during the four trying years where sorrow and suffering brought all Christians together. He was sent to Sandersville by the M. E. Conference and stayed with us from 1862 through 1867. Elsewhere I have told of the heroic work done by him and his coadjutors, Mr. Pincus Happ and Dr. James R. Smith, in confronting General Sherman.

In 1869, he re-established the camp meeting at Harris' Camp Ground. This was a notable event in the county. After a lapse of ten years, he was returned to Washington County to serve Tennille and Sandersville. It was at that time he edited for a while the newspaper owned by Mr. John Gilmore.

Mr. W. A. McCarty. Mr. William McCarty came to our county from Augusta in the fall of 1877. There was at that time not a brick store in Sandersville. Little wooden, one-story-buildings they were, with porches across the fronts. To go into a store, one had to go up from one to three steps, then across the porch into the store. These were poorly lighted by kerosene lamps or candles. Nothing daunted by conditions, Mr. McCarty, full of the energy which still characterizes him, rented a tiny building that stood where the Pastime Theatre now is. Later he purchased the corner, now occupied by Newman Brothers, and built the first brick store in town. The "Augusta Store," as Mr. McCarty named it, became known all over the county.

What Mr. McCarty was as a merchant, he was in every public interest, sparing neither time nor money to forward any enterprise he undertook. Through his determination when he became a member of the City Board of Education, he proposed and carried the measure to issue bonds for the first brick school building on our campus. He was the chairman of the water and light commission that constructed our water and light plant.

During the years of his activity, he was a promoter of the building of the Wrightsville and Tennille railroad, the Augusta Southern, the Sandersville Railroad, the Sandersville Enterprise Company, and organized the Farmers Oil and Guano Company.

C. R. Pringle. Mr. Pringle was a native of Barnesville. In 1861 he married Miss Nora Brantley, the only daughter of Mr. and Mrs. Harris Brantley, wealthy people who with several other families had moved in from their plantations and built homes in Sandersville.

In 1862 Mr. and Mrs. Pringle made Sandersville their home, as Mr. Pringle had entered the Confederate Army.

Quiet, dignified, conservative, until Reconstruction days, no one knew the hidden force of his character. It was in those trying times that he began his work of urging that the citizens develop Sandersville, and help Washington County to rise above the disasters of the war period. He opened a large general merchandise store, having only Washington County boys for clerks. Pringle's Store was known far and near.

Later, he served the county as a Legislator, next as Senator, then President of the Senate. He was one of the men who brought about the public school system for Sandersville. He and his father-in-law, Mr. Brantley, deeded to the city, some years previous to 1880 when Sandersville obtained a charter for the Public School, all the land upon which the Grammar School and the Vocational Building now stands, to be used for school purposes. He was a charter member of the City Board of Education, and served several years as President.

He was an earnest Christian, a steward in the Methodist Church, and for some years Superintendent of the Sunday School.

When high license was advocated, he became one of the leaders in the bitter fight we abstinence folks had with the liquor sellers, and those who wanted what they called "free liquor." When Washington County took up the cudgels to fight for Prohibition, he was at the head of the movement, working day and night, giving courage and advice to the younger men. Finally we won.

All through his life whatever was right, he did, never asking was a thing popular, but was it right? He was Mayor of the city, and did much to bring a more healthful condition by having low places drained or filled. When he retired from public life, time and again his advice was sought on matters of public welfare. He died of pneumonia on May 8, 1905.

John Rutherford settled in Washington County about four miles to the west of Sandersville. The Rutherford place is now owned by the heirs of Dr.

H. N. Hollifield. In the old family burial ground the original settler and his wife are buried. The Rutherfords in Georgia who have become famous as lawyers, teachers, and politicians are descendants of this John Rutherford.

Governor Charles J. Jenkins lived for three years in Sandersville. He was admitted to the bar here and practiced law in the early fifties.

Evan P. Howell was admitted to the bar in Sandersville and lived here in the late fifties. He enlisted in the Confederate service from Washington County and formed a company named Howell's Battery. After the war he returned to Sandersville and lived here several years, then moved to Atlanta, Georgia, where he became famous as the editor of the Constitution.

Oliver Prince, the author of "Polly Pea Blossom's Wedding," a writer of note in the fifties, spent some time in Washington County with his relatives, the Rutherfords.

Gen. Henry R. Jackson spent several summers of his early manhood in Washington County with the Rutherfords. He was the author of "The Red Old Hills of Georgia," and the hero of two wars, the Mexican War and the War Between the States.

Ex-Senator A. S. Clay was born in Washington County in the district that now bears the name of Clay. His parents moved away in the childhood of Senator Clay.

Captain J. W. Renfroe was a native of Washington County. He served in the War Between the States, being in all the great battles around Richmond, and returned to Sandersville at the close of the war. In 1872, he moved to Atlanta, and was Treasurer of the State of Georgia, and did much to straighten the finances of the State that had become so entangled in reconstruction days. Afterward, he was sent as U. S. agent to Alaska. He was faithful to every confidence reposed in him by the Government.

Col. Isaac Avery, author of the History of Georgia 1850-1881, lived several years in Sandersville.

Messrs. Enoch Clark and Morgan Jackson, besides being large land owners and successful farmers, were celebrated as surveyors. To them are due the accurate maps of the county.

The first Doolittle in the county was a **Mr. William Doolittle** from Connecticut. He was a teacher and located in the western part of the county where he taught in one of the chartered academies.

CHAPTER XVII.

PROMINENT MEN

Major E. A. Sullivan, for many years postmaster of Sandersville, was a Kentuckian by birth, a Georgian by adoption. He entered the Confederate Army in 1861, going to the front from Merriwether County. He located in Sandersville in 1867. He was very patriotic and believed in the development and advancement of the county. He was very learned, a great reader, had an unusual intellect well stored with knowledge and was beloved by all who knew him for his broad charity.

Judge Robert L. Rodgers' parents were Scotch Irish, who came from North Carolina about 1790 and settled over Buffalo on the Milledgeville road. The father of Judge Rodgers was a physician, one of the first in the county. He married a Miss Grier, who was closely related to Alexander H. Stephens. Judge Rodgers was an only child, every educational advantage was given him. He was a cadet in the State Military College when it was closed to enroll the boys into the Confederate Army. He saw service with such men as S. G. Jordan.

After the war he studied law and was a successful lawyer. All during the years he has written for various periodicals. He was for a long time Historian General for the Confederate Veterans. It has been truly said that he was more intimately acquainted with history than any man of his day. His articles on histories unfair to the South received close attention and were productive of much good in the school world. As an orator Judge Rodgers had few equals, as a story-teller of by-gone days he could hold an audience in close attention. From our County he moved to Atlanta. Two of his daughters live here, Mrs. S. G. Lang, Sr., and Mrs. John Lockhart. For a number of years Judge Rodgers has lived in Beaumont, Texas.

An amusing story of Buffalo Creek is told by Judge Rodgers, who says it was generally known in the Buffalo section. There was a man who lived near the creek by the name of Davis. He never permitted anything or anybody to "back him down." On one occasion he met a bull on the bridge. The bull would not let the man pass, but the man was determined to go over to the other side. So when the animal lowered his horns to charge, Mr. Davis caught him by the horns, twisted his neck and backed him into the water. After that, he was known as "Bull Davis." The lesson we may obtain from the story, when necessary stand your ground, even if it means meeting a difficulty as fierce as a bull.

Beverly Daniel Evans and his brother, **Thomas Evans**, were among the men who came in the early fifties to cast their lot with Washington County people. Both young men were lawyers.

Thomas Evans was born in the village of Marion, S. C., on the 20th of April, 1822. He received his early education at the Marion Academy and completed his collegiate course at William and Mary College, Williamsburg, Virginia. He read law and was admitted to practice at the bar of his State. For a number of years he resided in Marion, where he attained a high reputation as a lawyer and orator. Such was his standing in his profession and influence in South Carolina that he received the appointment from President Pierce, of District Attorney of the United States for the District of South Carolina, and took up his residence in Charleston. He was a man of great cultivation, possessing a broad and scholarly mind and sparklingly brilliant wit. On the occasion of one of the society functions in Charleston, it is said that he was presented to a very charming and beautiful widow by the name of Mrs. Evans. "Ah, Madam," said he, you are the lady in search of whom I have spent all but the best years of my life. I am most happy to meet you." During the War Between the States, he was engaged as the Purchasing Agent of the Confederate Government. On August 6, 1856, he was married to Miss Mary E. Lawson, the daughter of a wealthy Washington County planter. After the close of the war, he returned to Sandersville, where he renewed the practice of his profession, in which he was engaged till the time of his death, April 30, 1879.

Colonel Beverly Daniel Evans, Sr., was a native of Marion, S. C., and was born in 1826. He was admitted to the bar in 1847. He came to Sandersville to practice law in 1852. He had the polish and courtesy of the South Carolinian of the Old South. Well informed on all subjects of interest, thoroughly educated, an astute lawyer, he soon became one of the great lawyers of his time. He married first Miss Belle Smith, a daughter of Uncle Billie Smith. She died in a short while. His second wife was the sister of his first wife, Miss Sallie Smith. She was in truth a helpmeet. Their home life was ideal. They had seven sons, two died in youth, five are well known, not only in the county, but in the State as well, Judge Beverly D. Evans, Dr. Julian Evans, Messrs. George, Willis and Louis Evans, and one daughter, now Mrs. Alice Booz.

Col. Evans's war record (1861-65) was an enviable one. He was one of those who when Georgia seceded, organized a company. When it was mustered in, he had the rank of Captain. For bravery, he was given the rank of Colonel.

When the war closed, he again practiced his profession. He was for many years a member of the Board of Education. His profession, and his farming interests required all of his time, therefore he never actively entered politics.

General Thomas Jefferson Warthen was killed at Malvern Hill. He was one of the wealthy men of the long ago. For a while he lived near Warthen, then in Sandersville. Afterwards, he built Forest Grove, a beautiful place two miles east of town. General Warthen had built at Hamburg the first mill in Washington County.

Mr. Harris Brantley was another of the men of that day who owned much land and many servants. He was in every way a progressive man, high minded, right in word and deed.

Major Joseph Bangs was a scholar, a great reader, conversant with all the classics. His library, the finest in the county, was destroyed when the home was burned three weeks before Sherman arrived.

Judge Patrick Rose Taliaferro, a Virginian, came to Washington County in 1858. He was a charter member of the Phi Kappa Sigma Fraternity. His death leaves but one of the original members living, Dr. Bachman of Chattanooga. Judge Taliaferro came to our State for his health's sake. He found what he desired in the climate of Washington County. After living in Sandersville a year, he entered the Law School at the University of Georgia, 1859, graduated in 1861, and entered the Confederate Army immediately afterwards. He was married in March, 1862, to Miss Julia Smith, one of Uncle Billie Smith's daughters. He was soon promoted to captain, and was with the lost troops on Cheat Mountain, where they went seven days without food.

At the close of the war, he began farming near Sun Hill then moved to Sandersville. He was for a long time a drygoods merchant. He held the position of Treasurer on the original City Board of Education.

He was Judge of the County Court, and served several years as Treasurer of the county. For many years he was Moderator of Washington Baptist Association. He was the beloved Superintendent of the Baptist Sunday School for thirty-two years.

The love of temperance was imbued in him, even in boyhood he wrote and spoke on the subject. He helped in every move made by the total abstinence advocates and stood shoulder to shoulder with the other great men who gave their time, talents, and money to bring about first county, then State and finally National Prohibition. He died in 1919 beloved by all who knew him.

Samuel W. Lang, Henry C. Lang, and Isaiah Gilmore came in the early part of the nineteenth century from Portland, Maine, to build the Capitol at Milledgeville. All three were master builders. There was a fourth New Englander who worked with them, William Wadley. When the Capitol was finished, Sam. W. Lang and Isaiah Gilmore returned to Maine. Henry C. Lang and William Wadley remained to build the bridge over the Oconee River. At that time the river was the boundary between Baldwin and Washington. On the Washington side they erected a saw mill, the first in the County. Henry C. Lang married in Sandersville, Miss Nancy Davis. They were the parents of S. G. Lang, Sr.

When the Court House and the Masonic Hall were built, Mr. Henry Lang was one of the builders. He assisted William Wadley in the construction of the Central of Georgia Railroad. At that time Mr. Wadley was a resident of Washington County. He was the first President of the Central Railroad.

Drs. William P. Haynes, A. A. Cullens, James Rembert Smith were famous physicians of the days when Sandersville and Washington County were young.

Over Buffalo were **Dr. Tully Graybill, Dr. H. Hodges, Dr. R. Y. Rodgers, and Dr. Jared Irwin.** These men were all kept busy, the county was large and there was no means of conveyance, except horseback or buggy.

In the early part of the nineteenth century, **E. S. Langmade** came to Washington County from Canada. He had a large plantation, a grist mill and a brickyard about a mile from Sandersville.

Mr. Good Davis, maternal grandfather of S. G. Lang, Sr., came to Washington County as an Indian Scout before the county was laid out. He knew when the Creeks and Cherokees camped where Sandersville now is.

Stubbs Family. John Stubbs married Annie Wallace and came to Washington County from North

Carolina. Among his children were Gabriel Stubbs, whose children were John, William, Archie, Jasper, Frank, Edwin, Gabriel, Mary, Emma, Martha, Margaret, and Sarah.

John Stubbs owned a tract of land near Warthen which is now owned by James H. Hooks. The tract of land now owned by the Warthens and which holds the world's record for producing the greatest number of bales of cotton per acre was originally owned by John Stubbs, then given to Gabriel Stubbs, who sold it to Capt. William Warthen, the owner at the time it produced the record quantity of cotton.

Gabriel Stubbs reared four sons, each of whom served as Confederate soldiers during the entire period of the War between the States, these four being Archie, Jasper, Frank, and Edwin.

Emma Stubbs married Daniel Ainsworth, Mary married A. W. Stewart, Martha married W. H. Renfroe, Margaret married Mizel G. Wood, Jr., and Sarah married Charles M. Joyner.

Wood Family. George Wood and Harry Wood were brothers, born and reared in Washington County. The latter was the father of Dr. J. S. Wood who moved to Irwinton and reared a large family of children, among whom are Dr. Hubert Wood, Mrs.

Orian Manson, Mrs. Marvin Williams, Mrs. Dott Todd, Mrs. L. J. Pritchard and Mrs. George H. Carswell.

George Wood had three sons, Henry H., Franklin, and Jordan. Henry H. Wood lived all his life in the old Bay Springs Church community, in the eighty-eighth Militia District, and was for many years the Justice of the Peace in the district. He had a large family of six sons and four daughters, four of the sons were in the Confederate Army from the very beginning of that awful struggle in the sixties. Three of them were killed in battle, and the fourth one severly wounded, from which he suffered the remainder of his life. When the last call came, which took the old men and boys, Henry H. Wood himself enlisted.

He was the father of William T. Wood and Mizel G. Wood, Jr., the former being the father of James H. Wood, Samuel W. Wood and Gordon C. Wood, and the latter being the father of Newman Wood, E. Pierce Wood, Mrs. B. T. Rawlings, and J. Hines Wood.

J. Hines Wood is the present County Solicitor. He resigned his office as Solicitor of the City Court of

Sandersville to serve his country in the Great World War, rising to the rank of First Lieutenant, Eighteenth Machine Gun Battalion, American Expeditionary Forces. After returning from France, he was honorably discharged at Camp Devens, Mass., came back to his Washington County home, and in the next election that followed his return he was again honored by the people of the county with the election to the same office which he resigned to enter the war, being elected without opposition.

There were two Mizel Woods, M. G. Wood, Sr., being the father of Ernest C. Wood, Mrs. L. A. Graybill and Mrs. John E. Smith, and he was for several years the Tax Collector of Washington County.

Washington County, and particularly the old Eighty-eighth District, is the birthplace of many of the Wood family, some of them being Matthew K. Wood, Augustus Wood, William Wood, Robert Wood and Benjamin Wood, all staunch citizens and well-to-do farmers.

Among the children of Benjamin Wood are G. H. Wood, of Tennille, and W. J. Wood, who moved to Butts County.

J. S. Wood and Charles S. Wood were successful merchants at Oconee, from which place they moved to Savannah, and were brothers of A. W. J. Wood, one of whose sons, Wade H. Wood, was County School Commissioner for four years.

CHAPTER XVIII.

THE HEBREW CITIZENS OF OUR COUNTY

Among the men who did so much for the advancement and development of our county, none did more than several of those of the Israelitish nation, who in early days came to Washington County to make it their home.

Mr. Pincus Happ came from Europe in the middle of the nineteenth century. From New York he came South, leaving his family in that city until he could locate. In those days there were no stores in the country that sold good drygoods, and but few in the towns.

Mr. Happ went through the county, as did the dentists, from home to home selling drygoods. In the early fifties, he decided upon Sandersville in which to settle, brought his family there, and in 1859 opened a drygoods store.

As long as he lived his name was the synonym for all that was kind, helpful, and charitable. Many a person's hunger was appeased by his kindness. In sickness, or sorrow he was a friend. When Sherman had ordered Sandersville burned, Mr. Happ went with Rev. Anthony to beg for it to be spared.

He was succeeded in business and his works of benevolence were continued by his only son, Mr. Morris Happ, so well known in our county. Mr. Pincus Happ was too advanced in age to enter the Confederate Army, but his son was a Southern Soldier.

Mr. Happ like Major Mark Newman left his native country to cast his fortune with America, because of the persecutions in Poland.

Miss Jennie, his eldest daughter, married Mr. Bennett Hymes of New York; Miss Annie, the other daughter, was the wife of Mr. Louis Cohen.

Mr. Morris Happ was an honored citizen of the county, as well as the town. Everybody knew him, and hosts of people loved him. He was for a number of years a member of the City Board of Education, and at one time its president. He was the founder of the Happ Medal given for excellence in scholarship, and deportment, one was offered to every grade of the school. Even after he moved to Macon he gave the medals, until by an action of the Board of Education, all medals and prizes were abolished.

Mr. Lee Happ, the eldest son of Mr. Morris Happ, succeeded his father in business here and the name of Happ from 1859 until 1920 was known in the dry-goods world.

When Tennille was a small village, soon after railroad communication was restored with the outside world, there came to locate in Tennille a number of Poles. Among them were Mr. Sam Bashinski and family and his brother Louis. From that time until recently, their name as merchants and upbuilders of the community and county was almost a household word. Socially, politically, and financially they had great influence.

Many years ago Captain Isaac Hermann and his cousin, Abram, came to America from Alsace, Lorraine. Both of them lived for awhile in Davisboro, later Captain Hermann opened a store at Fenn's Bridge. When the call to arms in 1861 came, both of them offered for service to fight in the Southern Army, and they went through the war.

Captain Hermann in his quaint way told the enrolling officer: "I, a Frenchman, wish to fight like an American."

When the war closed, Mr. Abe Hermann went back to Davisboro where he was a merchant a long time, then moved his family to Mississippi.

Captain Hermann located in Sandersville where, except for a short while, he lived until his death a few years ago. He was an enthusiastic, wide awake, fearless man. For a long while he was on the Board of Education and served faithfully, doing everything to develop the system.

He wrote a very interesting account of his experience in the War of 1861-65, "The Memoirs of a Confederate Veteran." It is well worth the reading. Almost every one in the county knew "Captain Ike." He was for several terms Tax Receiver. He is survived by one daughter, Mrs. Henry Paris, and six sons, all of whom occupy positions of trust. Dr. Henry Hermann lives in Sandersville, and is a well known physician and surgeon.

Another man who helped to make Washington County what it is today is Mr. Henry Paris. In 1872 he came from Prussia to be free to live according to his conscience, for he did not like the militarism of his native land. He remained in New York until 1874, then came to Sandersville to be with his sister who was the wife of Mr. Morris Happ. He was an employee of P. Happ and Son until 1882, then he went to Eastman. He returned in 1889 and was a member of the firm of Cohen and Paris. At the death of the Cohen brothers, the firm was then formed into Happ and Paris.

Mr. Paris is not only known as a business man in Sandersville, but he has land interests in the county. He has always been a promoter of public affairs. He stands high as a Mason. He was for years on the City Board of Education and served several terms as President. Generous and just, he has hosts of friends, he is verily a friend in need. During the World War, no native Georgian was more devoted to the cause for which we fought than was Mr. Paris.

Among the men who have helped both the towns and the country is Mr. Louis Cohen. He is a native of Americus, Georgia, and as a young man was very popular in his home town. In 1877 sometime after his marriage to Miss Annie Happ, he came to Sandersville to live. He was young, full of enthusiasm, and determined to help his adopted town to grow.

From the time he came until the present day, he has worked faithfully for the advancement of every town or county interest.

Through his efforts the first cotton warehouse was built. He caused the first telephone service to be installed, including lines to Wrightsville and Tennille. He was the promoter of the telegraph line from Sandersville to Dublin. He was President of the Birmingham Guano Company which had an office here. He built the ginnery and flour mills, afterwards owned by Wiley Harris and Sons.

He built the short line railroad between Sandersville and Tennille, after the first road had been purchased by the Augusta Southern.

For thirty years he was a member of the City Board of Education, for eleven years its President, always kind and considerate of the teachers, and deeply interested in the pupils, he was greatly beloved by them.

Another honor conferred upon him was the mayoralty of Sandersville. Mr. Cohen has two children, Mr. H. E. Cohen of Atlanta, Mrs. I. B. Lieberman of Sandersville.

The life of **Major Mark Newman**, full of eventful incidents, deserves a permanent record. He was a native of Poland and came to this Country in 1845. In 1861 he enlisted in the Confederate Army and served with distinction in the Forty-ninth Georgia Regiment and was promoted to the rank of adjutant.

He war ordinary of Wahington County from 1881 until his death in 1903. He was devoted to his official duties, and was beloved by the veterans and widows who received pensions from the county.

He was one of the most popular, most widely known and loved of men who ever lived in our county. He was a modest man, and never pressed forward his own good deeds in a spirit of vain glory. He was kind. He was generous. He was charitable.

He married Miss Ann Ainsworth, a member of one of the very good families of Washington County. Two sons, J. D. Newman and I. W. Newman, survive them and for many years have been successful merchants in Sandersville.

CHAPTER XIX.

PROMINENT MEN

Dr. H. N. Hollifield was born in Maryland. He came to Sandersville in 1855, the death of several of the older physicians leaving a good opening for a young man to begin practicing medicine. Dr. Hollifield was a graduate of a Philadelphia college where he obtained his literary degrees. His M. D. degree was from Jefferson Medical College, Philadelphia.

From the time he located in Washington County to the day of his death, it was his own by adoption and no man ever lived who was more loyal to the town and the county than he. He was broad minded, deep thinking, thoroughly educated, a ready writer, a finished speaker, and had a wonderful memory.

His practice was extensive. He literally worked himself to death, sometimes going day and night without sleep. Faithful to his profession he could never refuse a call, although he knew he would receive no compensation. It is told of him that he frequently, at the close of the war, when he came home from service, would walk several miles to see a patient. On one occasion he walked to Oconee, because the messenger who came for him was riding a poor mule. You must remember that the railroad had been destroyed and there were no horses to be bought.

Dr. Hollifield was great, not only as a physician, but as a school-man also. In 1871 when the Public School System was adopted for Georgia, he was asked to become Superintendent of the County Schools. He agreed to do the work for the love of it. It is said that when he had to visit a patient near a school he always made it convenient to call by to see the school and the teacher. In that way he knew conditions well. He was in the position of County Superintendent for twenty-five years. He was one of the promoters of the Public School for Sandersville, and served on the Board of Education from 1880 until his death.

As a Mason, he was one of the brightest in the State. Like Thomas Jefferson, he believed in covering people's faults with the broad mantle of Christian Charity.

Progressive in thought, he was always ready to do everything for the advancement of the people of the county. He spent his time, talent, and money for the betterment of this section.

When the call to arms came in 1861, he was ready. He organized an artillery company as the roster of the county shows.

Possibly the greatest of his work was done for the cause of Temperance. Early and late with tongue and pen, with time and money, he helped fight the good fight that made Washington County dry. His life work ended in 1895.

Judge Beverly D. Evans. Of her famous men, we doubt that any man ranked higher in the estimate of the citizenry of the State than Beverly D. Evans II. He was born in 1865, reared in Sandersville, finished school under Prof. Ivy W. Duggan and Capt. Hugh Lawson.

He graduated at Mercer University, then took his degree in law at Yale. He began the practice of law with his father in Sandersville. He was elected to the State Legislature when barely twenty-one. His colleague was Col. C. R. Pringle. They both fought valiantly for county prohibition and had the pleasure of seeing Washington County the first one to go dry.

Judge Evans was the youngest man to sit on the bench of the Superior Court. He was Judge of the Middle Circuit for a number of years, then he was elected to the Superior Court Judgeship of Georgia. When he resigned to take the Federal Court Judgeship of the Eastern Circuit, he was next to the Chief Justice of the State.

Whatever gift was in the power of the people of Washington County to bestow he could have had it, but he never desired political honors.

As friend, brother, husband, father, or citizen he was ideal. Like Sir Galahad, spiritually he had the power of ten men, because his life was pure. In Washington County's galaxy of great names, his is a star of the first magnitude.

PROMINENT MEN WHO LIVED NEAR WARTHEN

The Sparks family, once a large number of brothers and sisters, whose progenitor was Thomas Sparks, have all gone into the Beyond. The last one who lived in Georgia was **Mr. Thomas H. Sparks**, so long a resident of Sandersville. He occupied various positions of trust, for several terms he was treasurer of the county. He was a member of the City Board of Education. He was a veteran of the War Between the States. He and two of his brothers were in the battle of Gettysburg, one of which, Mr. George Sparks, was killed there, and was buried on the field of battle by his brothers.

Closely allied to the Sparks were the Mathis family, men and women of sterling worth. None of the older generation survive. **Dr. A. Mathis** lived for many years in Sandersville. He was a successful physician and druggist.

The Adams family were another large family, at one time residents of the county. Like the Sparks and Mathises, they too had United States grants to their lands, and were all staunch, loyal citizens.

The Gilmores and Smiths were among the earliest settlers of the county, coming from Virginia as early as 1792. Their descendants are among the most progressive men of old Washington.

Mr. Leven Matthews moved to Washington County in the childhood of his son, **William C. Matthews**, who became one of the best citizens Washington County ever had. He was graduated from Emory

College as the war of 1861 came on. He enlisted from Washington County, was promoted to a captaincy in the Thirty-eighth Georgia Regiment. He suffered the hardships of prison life on Johnson's Island, Ohio.

After the war he secured the office of Revenue Tax Collector. In 1890-92 he represented the Twentieth District as State Senator. For twenty-two years he was agent of the Central R. R. in Tennille. He was, forty years ago, as progressive a farmer as we have now. He owned several places around Tennille, and above Sandersville. Kind, considerate, loyal, faithful to his county and State, above all to his church, he merits a place in the history of the county.

CHAPTER XX.

MEN OF WASHINGTON COUNTY WHO HAVE HELPED TO MAKE IT FAMOUS

Charles J. Bayne, only son of Mrs. S. J. Bayne of Sandersville, is now editor of the Macon Evening News. Though born in Milledgeville, he was brought here by his mother when three years old and began his life work in Washington County. His first position was in the Progress office when a boy of fifteen, then he went to Augusta and was in the office of the Chronicle, he next worked for the Herald. Then he was on the editorial staff of the Atlanta Journal, next on that of the Georgian. His fame as a paragrapher and as a writer went beyond the bounds of the State, for he accepted an offer from the Baltimore News. Thence he went to the Washington Post, finally to Macon. He is a student, a writer, an orator. Of his literary career we are justly proud.

Stanford E. Moses, now Admiral Moses, is from Washington County. His parents lived in the Boatright settlement below Tennille. He graduated from

Annapolis, the United States Naval Academy, when he was nineteen and saw his first service on the Oregon when the United States had some trouble with Chile. He was in the Spanish American War, later in the Phillipines, and finally in the World War.

John G. Harrison, D. D., is a native of Washington County. He was educated in academic work in his home town, Tennille. He entered Mercer in 1886 under a corps of able professors, headed by Dr. A. J. Battle. After graduation, he was Principal of Hiawassee High School, North Georgia, for four years. Then he spent several years in preparation for the ministry. Afterwards he preached for five years in the Baptist Church of Macon, Georgia. Then he resigned to go abroad for study and travel. On returning from the East he was elected to the Chair of Philosophy in Mercer University where he still is.

Already mention has been made of some of the men of an older generation who helped make Washington County famous. Among the men of Sandersville after the days of reconstruction was **Col. R. L. Warthen**, who was conceded by everybody to be the most learned man of his day. Quiet and retiring, only those who knew him best, realized what a store of knowledge he possessed. As a lawyer, he was astute, as a friend, loyal, sympathetic and kind. His brother, Mr. Macon Warthen, was to his home town, Warthen, what Col. Lee Warthen was to Sandersville.

Mr. C. I. Duggan's ancesors came to Washington County shortly after the Revolution and settled near Warthen. Mr. Duggan came to Sandersville in the late 70's. He was associated in business for several years with Mr. B. J. Tarbutton. Everybody a few years ago knew Tarbutton and Duggan's General Merchandise Store. Later Mr. Duggan withdrew from business life and devoted himself to farming.

Among the worthwhile sturdy men of our county was **Mr. Wiley Harris.** He had large landed interests in the western part of Washington County. In order to educate his sons and his only daughter he and his excellent wife moved into town, and built a home in West End. He and one son opened a large business in Sandersville, later he became owner of the large flour mill and steam ginnery located on Mill Street. Mr. Harris held the admiration and respect of the entire town for his integrity and upright life. His sons, Messrs. Dan, Walter, J. J. and

Dr. Eugene Harris are among our best citizens of the present generation.

Mr. B. J. Tarbutton came to Sandersville when a youth, directly after the War Between the States. Born and reared in the county, he was well known. With the exception of a very few years that were spent in merchandizing at Oconee, he was identified with everything for the advancement of his town and county. Naturally very timid and seclusive, few really knew what he did for the upbuilding of society and for the good of the town.

When the struggle for prohibition came, he worked earnestly for the right, sparing neither time nor money to bring about that which would rid the county of its greatest curse. True to his convictions, he was as fearless as he was quiet, ever willing to sacrifice his own interests for the cause of righteousness. When he died the poor and afflicted lost a friend.

Directly after the war, in 1865, a Savannah youth, **Charles C. Parsons,** came to Sandersville. He had been four years in the service of the South. He made his home in Sandersville, clerking at first for his uncle, Dr. Elijah Parsons, then for Mr. George D.

Warthen in whose employ he was when he died. Everybody loved Charles Parsons, always happy, ever ready to do a favor, a man whose word was his bond. Whatever was to be done for his adopted town he was ready to do it. He was ever the children's friend.

Judge Ben T. Rawlings finished school under the teaching of Dr. A. C. C. Thompson. He next graduated from Emory College. Afterwards he had his training in law at the University of Georgia. Like all men of great minds, he was quiet and unassuming in manner. Before he entered politics he was considered one of the foremost lawyers of the Middle Circuit. For several terms he was Solicitor of the Middle Circuit, then Legislator, afterwards for years Judge of the Superior Court. He was considered one of the most fearless, just, able judges that ever sat on the bench. Criminals feared his decisions, good citizens admired him.

In his home he was an ideal host, a cultured Southerner. As a father and husband, he was kind and loving, as a friend loyal. His farming interests were large, his laborers were devoted to him. He was Mayor of his home town, a member of the Board of

Education, for some time its President. When he found his health failing he resigned the judgeship, and devoted himself to the law.

What a galaxy of names there are that belong to the past of our county. Of course many of them are identified with Sandersville, because it was then the only large town and the county site. Many of these men lived and worked a hundred years ago.

'Uncle Billie Smith,'' whose father came when the Warthens, the Wickers, Cummings and others migrated from the Carolinas and Virginia, was one of the outstanding men. By inheritance and by industry he became very wealthy. He owned, when freedom came to the negroes, three hundred and fifty slaves. He was a kind master, a good husband, and a father devoted to his children. In our day, he would be called a constructionist, for he believed in building up the community. The brick building, now the Nurses' Home, was built by him for a hotel, the first brick structure in town. He owned carpenters, brick masons and other artisans, so when the Methodist Church was to be built, he offered to do it. He owned much property. ''Uncle Billie Smith'' was a generous, broad-minded man. He died during reconstruction days.

Judge James S. Hook, State School Commissioner in 1890-1896, was a resident of Washington County for years. He was a noted lawyer, and a Judge of the Superior Court. He married a Miss Emmie Harris, a Washington County girl. Dr. Hook, father of Judge Hook, was a physician in Sandersville in the fifties. It was through his influence that the Church of the Disciples (Christian) was established in the county.

Rev. Thomas M. Harris was a wealthy planter and a minister. He was born and reared in Washington County. He served several churches (Christian) in the county for years without any pay. He said he did not need the money, but the people did need the gospel. At his own expense he erected a church edifice on the border of Washington and Johnson Counties. He was one of the great preachers of his denomination, one of the profound thinkers of the past. He was a man of powerful intellect, which he developed thoroughly. He possessed a keen sense of humor, and he was very popular. He should be counted as one of the great men of Washington County.

C. D. Thigpen was for many years identified with the farming interests in the eastern part of the county. After the death of his father-in-law, Mr. Enoch Clarke, he had that property also to manage. He was the only railroad agent that Sunhill ever had. Mr. Thigpen was one of the most popular men the county ever had. Genial, kind, and honest, he invited confidence by his manner.

He was politically strong, but stronger still in the councils of his chosen church, for he was an official of the Washington Association in the Baptist Church for years. No man was more beloved than he by the veterans and the widows of the Confederacy. Possibly he was the only man in the county that could have taken Major Newman's place as Ordinary, and have carried on the work in as acceptable a manner.

CHAPTER XXI.

PROMINENT WOMEN

In the long ago, women were never prominent in political or business life as they are today. A woman was essentially a home-keeper. Therefore, for nearly a hundred years after our county was set off, the only position open to her was teaching, and very few Southern women up to 1860 even thought of that profession.

Your great-grandmothers and grandmothers were busy in the home, directing and ordering the work to be done. There were no conveniences then as now, no stores with shelves filled with canned food, no bakers bread, and just think! No stoves, no lamps, and all the spinning and weaving were done in the home.

The single women perfected themselves in housekeeping, sewing and embroidering, because the negro women, provided the family owned any, spun and wove. If these single aunts, cousins, and sisters did not marry, well, they lived at home with their parents.

People were content at home in those days. Even in the towns there was very little visiting. The children always found mother at home. So, you see, from 1784 until 1850 in our county there were no prominent women, from our view-point. One result of the war 1861-65, was that women bereft of fathers, husbands, sons and brothers, had to become teachers, dressmakers, or boarding-house keepers, or managers of their farms.

A woman known all over our county was **Miss Mary Walker Perry,** the first woman to open a store in Washington County. Connected with some of the best families, she soon had a large list of customers. At first she operated her sales-room in her home in Sandersville.

Mrs. Mary Franklin, widow of Sam O. Franklin, and mother of H. M. Franklin of Tennille, at the close of the war opened a boarding house in Tennille. She was widely known for her Southern hospitality and the very excellent house she kept. In sickness and sorrow she was an angel of mercy, not only in Tennille, but anywhere in the county.

In 1870 a young woman opened a little school in Tennille. Many of the older citizens recall with pleasure **Miss Maria Brookins Haynes**, one of the best primary teachers in Georgia. She was reared in Sandersville, and when Messrs. Duggan and Lawson opened their school in the latter place, she began teaching with them and taught the boys and girls of the county their "a, b, c's." She went into the Public School when it was organized in 1880 and taught there for more than a quarter of a century.

In the spring of 1873, the Ladies Memorial Association was formed as suggested by Mrs. Mary Ann Williams of Columbus. The President of the Association in our county was Mrs. B. D. Evans, Sr., closely associated with her were such women as Mrs. John Huff, Mrs. Thomas E. Brown, Mrs. Mack Jernigan and Mrs. S. J. Bayne. Later younger women took up the active work: Mrs. B. J. Tarbutton, Mrs. B. T. Rawlings, Mrs. W. C. Matthews, Mrs. C. D. Hardwick, Mrs. James D. Franklin and others.

Mrs. B. D. Evans was Miss Sallie Smith, daughter of Uncle Billie Smith. She was a woman of a strong intellect, thoroughly educated, a cultured gentlewoman. She was enthusiastic in her defense of the Lost Cause, and in order to imbue the young people with a love for the Southland and to perpetuate the memory of those who fell in battle, she worked early and late to erect a monument to the Confederate dead. At first a wooden cross was placed on the brow of the hill in the City Cemetery. Some years later through her influence, assisted by the Ladies Memorial Association, she succeded in having the cross replaced by the marble column that now stands on the spot.

Mrs. Evans was one of the charter members of the W. C. T. U. and held the office of President. In her church she was a power. Like the Roman matron, Cornelia, she pointed to her sons as her jewels, for she was the mother of U. S. Judge Beverly D. Evans, and the Evans brothers whom you all know.

Closely associated with Mrs. Evans was **Mrs. T. E. Brown,** known to her intimate friends as "Miss Fannie Brown." She too loved the South, especially her native county. She was a sister of Rev. Thomas J. Adams, the noted teacher and preacher. Her work was always for God, Home, and Native Land.

Mrs. A. J. Jernigan was a daughter of Dr. A. C. C. Thompson. Wherever there was a need "Aunt Fannie" was there. A tireless worker she never wearied in organizing and helping children. She formed the third in the trio of great women, who did so much for Washington County, not politically, but socially and morally. All of them worked hard for total abstinence, and began the movement that ended in our county becoming dry in 1886.

Of our notable women of the recent past **Mrs. B. J. Tarbutton,** known to those closely atached to her as "Mamie Bangs" heads the list. As mother and friend she was ideal in public service. She was a leader with "a man's mind and a woman's might." For twenty years she was a State official in the mission work of her church, the M. E. Church, South.

When the young men and a few young women undertook to rid Sandersville and Washington County of the liquor curse away back in the 70's, she was a faithful lieutenant under the leadership of older people, righteous men and women who planned, while younger ones fought. Her pen and mind were always at work. When W. C. T. U. was introduced into Georgia, Mrs. Tarbutton was offered the presidency of the Union here. She was called the lawyer of Women's conventions, for she could so quickly and clearly explain disputed points. But in sickness, trouble, and sorrow is where she proved herself "a gentle woman, nobly planned, to comfort, strengthen or command."

CHAPTER XXII.

WOMEN'S CLUBS

It has been said that Washington County could truly boast of more intellectual women than any other county in the State. To prove the statement, a person has but to investigate the amount of mental work accomplished by them in the last decade in every section of the county, and ten years merely records the work of the younger women.

We can go back a generation and find the same condition true. First, there were those who worked so faithfully for Memorial Day, under the name of the Ladies Memorial Association. Then the U. D. C., next the W. C. T. U., and now Federation is the magic word.

FEDERATED CLUBS OF WASHINGTON COUNTY

Sandersville Music Study Club, President, Miss Ruth Gaines, organized and federated 1923, members nineteen.

Sisters Community Club, Sandersville, R. F. D., President, Mrs. J. L. Champion, organized 1919, federated 1921, members 20.

Woman's Club, Warthen, President, Mrs. T. R. Duggan, organized and federated 1920, members 18.

Fine Arts Club, Tennille, President, Miss Louise Brown, organized and federated 1920, members 30.

Woman's Club, Tennille, President, Mrs. Wilbur Smith, organized 1914, federated 1915, members 166.

Round Table Club, Sandersville, President, Mrs. A. W. Evans, organized and federated 1910, members 16.

Sorosis Club, Sandersville, President, Mrs. R. L. Smith, organized and federated 1922, members 21.

Transylvania Club, President, Mrs. Arthur A. Rawlings, organized 1910, federated 1920, members 30.

Washington County Federation, President, Mrs. A. A. Rawlings, organized and federated 1920, members 345.

Woman's Club, Sandersville, President Mrs. Hovey Smith, organized and federated 1919, members 60.

SISTER'S COMMUNITY CLUB

The Sisters' Community Club was named for the old church, Sisters' Church, which was organized in 1850. Undoubtedly one of the livest, most progressive clubs to be found anywhere is the Sisters' Community Club. Organized as a Canning Club in 1919, it became federated in 1921, and has every department of work that those in the cities have.

The first President of the club was Mrs. Ben R. Tanner, one of the most intellectual, practical, well balanced women in Washington County. Under her wise administration the club grew and developed.

The report of 1921-1922 showed from the sale of butter, eggs, chickens, home-cured meats, sausage, lard, cream, milk, vegetables, and fruits, a net sum of $5,246.47. This was not put into the club treasury, but each individual used her portion for her own household.

Prize after prize was won at different fairs, even in the State fair. All this money went into the club treasury. The motto of the club is "We Can." The members voted to sponsor schools, to aid in improving school buildings, and to furnish clothing for destitute children. The club was represented in both Athens and Savannah at conferences.

Mr. L. Clayton Matthews, now of Atlanta, but a Washington County boy, has donated land opposite Sisters' Church upon which the club will erect a club house, which is to be a social center for the community.

In Sisters' Church Community for the past twelve years has lived one of the finest artists in Georgia, a woman who has studied abroad, as well as a graduate from some of the best colleges in the United States. Gentle, cultured, refined, **Miss Elizabeth Matthews** enjoys the quiet, peaceful home life of Mr. and Mrs. John F. Tanner. Both Mrs. Tanner and her sister, Miss Matthews, are Georgians. Their home was in Atlanta, now they are adoptions of Washington County. With her pictures, her books, and her flowers, Miss Matthews leads the ideal life of an artist.

THE TRANSYLVANIA CLUB

The Transylvania Club was organized by Mrs. C. B. Chapman at her home on October 23, 1918. There were eighteen girls present. The purpose of the club, as stated by the organizer, was for mental development and social intercourse. Miss Mary Tarbutton was elected President, Miss Ethel Elder, Vice-President and Miss Mary Stephens Irwin, Secretary. The motto chosen was: "Service, not for Ourselves but for Others."

In January, 1909, at a meeting in the home of Dr. and Mrs. A. J. Irwin, the Transylvanians began the organization of a library. This was at the suggestion of Miss Mary Tarbutton, who had recently returned from a visit to a friend, who was a librarian in Passaic, N. J. The Sandersville Public Library was opened March 11, 1909 by a book shower. The club rented the lower floor of the Masonic building. Finally, by contributions from friends, dinners given by the club, entertainments by home talent, there were seven thousand books on the shelves. When the disastrous fire occurred in February, 1920, destroying all the books except about two dozen, the devoted Transylvanians went to work with indomitable will, and phenix-like from the ashes they succeeded in re-establishing the library and have accumulated between two and three thousand volumes.

Miss Mary Tarbutton (now Mrs. Robert Freeman) was librarian from 1909 until her marriage in 1921.

Miss Fannie Lou Irwin was the first Treasurer and still holds the position as Mrs. Findlay Irwin. Both ladies have evidenced unusual executive ability, and the club as a unit has supported them in all they have done. Since Mrs. Freeman lives in California, Miss Sadie Tarbutton has been elected to the position of Librarian and Miss Gladys Dukes, Assistant Librarian.

ROUND TABLE CLUB

In 1910, the Round Table Club was organized by a group of young matrons of Sandersville. Their desire was two-fold: first, a closer personal acquaintance, sympathetic conference, and systematic training; the second desire was self-improvement, which can be accomplished only by study and discussion. Early in its existence it was federated. Mrs. E. P. Wood was its first President. The motto chosen was "Unity and Diversity," its flower, the pink rose. The membership was limited to sixteen.

THE TWENTIETH CENTURY CLUB

The Twentieth Century Club is the oldest existing Literary Club in Sandersville. Its organizer was Miss Emily West, who in 1907 called a few intimate friends together to discuss a course of study that would mean intellectual growth and mutual improvement. Its first President was Miss Emily West. Its meetings are held bi-monthly. The number of members was limited to fourteen active members and six honorary members. On its list have been the names of some of the most intellectual women of the town.

THE SOROSIS CLUB

This is the infant of the group of clubs formed by the women of Sandersville. It was organized in 1922 and the purpose was intimate association and hard study. Realizing the importance of federation, soon after it was organized it was federated as "The Baby of the Tenth District.''

The first President was Mrs. R. L. Smith, noted for her executive ability.

D. A. R.

The Governor Jared Irwin Chapter Daughters of American Revolution was organized in 1910. Mrs. Dan C. Harris was the first Regent.

In order to foster a love of history, the Chapter offered a prize to the pupil in the High School who made the best yearly record in American History. After some years the Board of Education forbade the offering of prizes or medals, so the Chapter withdrew their offer.

They have discovered all graves of Revolutionary soldiers in their division of the county and marked those that had no marking stones, as follows:

1. James Gilmore, buried on Sandersville road near Warthen.

2. William Warthen, buried at Hamburg, near Warthen.

3. John Sparks, buried nine miles north of Sandersville.

4. John Lawson Irwin, buried near Tennille.

5. William Irwin, buried near Tennille.

6. Alexander Irwin, buried near Tennille.

7. Jared Irwin, buried near Tennille.

8. William Hood, buried near Warthen.

9. Andrew Thompson Lawson, buried near Oconee.

10. John Rutherford, buried on Hollifield place.

11. William Gainer, buried on Gainer place near Davisboro.

CHAPTER XXIII

IMPROVED CONDITIONS IN THE COUNTY

There is much to say in contradiction of those who claim that our county is not improved by the Prohibition Law. From old newspapers, from records kept by our fore-parents, from tradition and from personal observation, we know that conditions are much better, very much better. At every cross roads was one at least of those disreputable places called "groggeries," and at each one occurred, some of the most atrocious crimes listed in any catalogue, most frequent of which were cold blooded murders. Conditions grew worse and worse until just before the War Between the States, a Temperance wave swept over this section. Then, many drunkards were reformed and reclaimed, and Christian men and women were brought together to fight the evil.

A few of the noted men of those days were Rev. T. J. Adams, a noted Baptist, Rev. J. J. Hyman, Messrs. Nimrod Pitman, Owen Pope, Sr., Simon

Hood, Sherod Hood, Martin Morgan, Lawson Davis, and James Rushin. To these can be added many names of famous men and women of that time. Young men became great orators on Temperance problems.

Later came Dr. H. N. Holifield of Maryland, Dr. G. W. H. Taliaferro of Virginia, Beverly D. Evans of South Carolina, E. A. Sullivan of Greene County, C. R. Pringle of Pike County. All of these newcomers lent their aid to the old residents to help control the saloon when issues were made. All this created public sentiment. The grog-shop disappeared, but the barroom remained a curse. It was a hindrance to everything uplifting. Murders were frequent. In the towns, street duels and sometimes free-for-all fights occurred.

The Temperance lodges, blazing the way for better things, had their day. Then came to the front, such men as Bradford Roughton, Charlie Mitchell, Ben Tarbutton, Thomas J. Davis, backed by men of such faith and ability as those above mentioned, and seconded by Wash Kilpatrick, Thomas Adams, A. J. Battle, George M. Clark, Thomas M. Harris, A. G. Thomas, J. J. Hyman, all ministers. The editors were with us, the Christian women stood squarely by the men. A youth, Beverly D. Evans, Jr. (later Georgia's great Temperance Judge, on the Supreme bench, later of the Federal Court) used his wonderful gift of oratory, and with his colleague, Col. C. R. Pringle, in the Legislature made Washington County dry.

The history of this tremendous struggle would fill volumes, and then it could not convey in full the brain power, heart agony, every talent of tongue and pen used. Neither can all the names of the workers be chronicled. However, these come to our mind in addition to those mentioned: Cols. John N. Gilmore, Steve J. Jordan, Oscar Rogers, John N. Rogers, Messrs. Thomas Evans, Jr., Thomas H. Sparks, Dr. M. D. C. M. Summerlin. These spoke and worked day and night through the County. When the test came, four bar-keepers voted the dry ticket. At Oconee one of them placed this placard over the door, "Away with liquor and save the people." After this Georgia went dry, then came National Prohibition. Of course, the law is broken, what law is not? The Ten Commandments are daily transgressed, but we need them. To Hon. C. R. Pringle is indisputably accredited the honor of being the Father of Prohibition in Georgia. He was not a fanatic, but a cool, clear-headed business man, who made a success of whatever he undertook. Had he tried, he could have made a success in National Councils.

It is left in the hands of the youth of our county to move forward along the path of righteousness made safe for them.

CONCLUSION

This little volume is written by one who is an amateur in the work of being an author. She has done the best she could for the love she bears to the children of the county, hoping that from the truths chronicled, they may imbibe a love for their section, and that they will do everything in their power to make it the very best county of the State. Quoting Walter Scott:

"I know not how true the tale may be,
I tell it to you as it was told to me."

(THE END.)

INDEX

ADAMS	144	
. FANNIE	157	
. T.J.	75,168	
. THOMAS	169	
. THOMAS J.	157	
AINSWORTH	96	
. ANN	139	
. DANIEL	129	
. EMMA STUBBS	129	
ALDRED	55	
. A.W.	55	
ANDREW	105	
ANTHONY,	64	
	66-67,134	
. BASCOM	115	
. JAMES	64	
. JAMES D.	27,115	
AUDUBON	14	
AVANT, A.S.	58	
. GERTRUDE	104	
. JOSEPH	10,82	
AVERY, ISAAC	120	
BACHMAN	126	
BAILEY	54	
. W.G.	55	
BANGS,		
. JOSEPH	73,81,126	
BARKSDALE	19	
BARNETT,		
. ABRAHAM	11	
BASHINSKI,		
. JULIUS	87	
LOUIS	135	
. SAM	135	
BASHINSKY,		
. HERMANN	87	
BATTLE, A.J.	147,169	
BAYNE		
. CHARLES J.	146	
. S.J.	146,156	
BEACH, ASA	90	
BEALL	55	
. O.H.P.	55	
BEAM	34	
BECK, T.J.	42	
BEDDINGFIELD,		
. JOSEPH	82	
BEDINGFIELD, J.	10	
BELL	19,64	
. AUGUSTUS	74, 79	
. GREEN	62	
. W.A.	62,79	
BENTON	50	
BERRIEN	19	
BOATRIGHT,		
. B.S.	50,101	
. BEN S.	44	
BOOZ		
. ALICE EVANS	125	
BRANTLEY	19,30,57	
. FRANK	62	
. GREEN	73	
. HARRIS	29,117,125	
. NORA	117	
BROOKINS, ELLA	29	
. HAYWOOD	73	
. HEYWARD	86	
BROOKS	19	
BROWN, CLEM	46	
. CLEM C.	86	
. FANNIE ADAMS	157	
. LOUISE	161	
. SIDNEY	91	
. T.E.	157	
. THOMAS E.	35	
	70,156	
BRYAN	53	
BULLARD	19	
. LEWIS	43	
BURNETT	19,104	
BURNEY, J.	10	
. JOHN	82	
BURR, AARON	21	
BUSH, THOMAS	11	
CARSWELL,		
. GEORGE H.	130	
CARTER	70	
CASON	103	
CHAMPION	99	
. J.L.	161	
CHANDLER,		
. WILLIAM	50	
CHAPMAN,		
. C.B.	81-82,163	
CHEATHAM	54,113	
. A.L.	55	
. A.T.	112	
. D. LOUIS	112	
. D.L.	55,109	
CHRISTMASS,		
. ROBERT	11	
CLARK, ENOCH	120	
. GEORGE M.	169	
. MILTON	103	
CLARKE, ENOCH	153	
CLAY,, A.S.	120	
COBB	19	
COFIELD	62	
COHEN	137	
. ANNIE HAPP	134	
.	137	
. H.E.	138	
. LOUIS	26, 86	
.	134,137	
COLLINS	70	
COOK, TOM	45	
COOLEY	103	
CRAFTON,		
. S. BENNETT	80	
CRAWFORD	19	
CULLEN	19	
CULLENS	93	
. A.A.	128	
. AUGUSTUS A.	73	
CUMMING, T.J.	74-75	

INDEX

CUMMINGS	151	
DANIEL	103-104	
. JOHN	10 82	
. WILLIAM	11	
DAVIS	19,64,122	
. BULL	123	
. GOOD	128	
. JEFFERSON	22	
. LAWSON	169	
. NANCY	127	
. PORTER	45	
. T.J.	54	
. THOMAS	J.,74,169	
DEASON	64	
DENNARD,		
. JACOB	10,82	
DENNIS, JACOB,	10	
DOOLITTLE,		
. GEORGE	85	
. WILLIAM	120	
DUGGAN	78,156	
. C.I.	148	
.ELIZ. WALKER	76	
. IVY W.,29,74-77,142		
. JAMES R.	77	
. MELL L.	77	
. T.R.	161	
. W.L.	42	
DUKES,GLADYS,	165	
DYKES,W.F.,	42	
ELBERT		
. SAMUEL	46,48-49	
ELDER,ETHEL,	164	
ELKINS,	56,104	
EMANUEL		
. DAVID	113	
ENGLISH, W.M.	85	
EVANS	28,124,143	
. A.W.	161	
. ALICE	125	
. B.D.	35,70,81,156	
. BELLE SMITH	124	

. BEVERLY D.	90,125	
.	142,157,169-170	
. BEVERLY		
. DANIEL	123-124	
. GEORGE	61,125	
. J.H.	55	
. JULIAN	55,110,125	
. LOUIS	61,125	
. MARY E.		
. LAWSON	124	
. R.J.	53	
. SALLIE		
. SMITH	124,156	
. THOMAS	81,123	
.	170	
. WILLIS	61,125	
EVERETT	104	
FENN	49,89	
FISH,		
. MAMIE HINES	111	
. WILLIAM	111	
FLOURNOY	64,93	
FLOYD,		
. J.U.	35	
. SILAS	35	
FLUKER	19	
FRANKLIN	48	
. BENJAMIN	9	
. GEORGE	11,48-50	
. H.M.	50,155	
. HERBERT M.	46	
. HERBERT		
. MITCHELL	46	
. J.D.	39	
. JAMES D.	46,48	
.	156	
. MARY	155	
. P.	10	
. PHILEMON	82	
. S.O.	50	
. SAM O.	41,43,155	

. WILLIAM	50	
FREEMAN	165	
. MARY		
. TARBUTTON	164	
. ROBERT	164	
FULGHUM	5	
. W.H.	53	
GAINER	54	
. WILLIAM	51,167	
GAINES,RUTH	160	
GALPHIN,		
. GEORGE	10	
GILMER	19	
GILMORE	144	
. ISAIAH	127	
. JAMES	167	
. JOHN	115	
. JOHN N.	81,170	
. MARY MILDRED	36	
GLADDIN,L.A.	58	
GRAYBILL	56	
. L.A.	131	
. TULLY	70,128	
GRESHAM		
. DAVID	11	
GRIER	121	
. DAVID	19	
. WILLIAM	11	
HAINES,		
. NATHANIEL	73	
HALL	54	
. J.L.	100	
HAPP	65,134	
. ANNIE	134,137	
. JENNIE	134	
. LEE	135	
. MORRIS	134-135	
.	137	
. P.	137	
. PINCUS	64,115	
.	133,134	

INDEX

HARDEE	68	. ISAAC 55,135
HARDWICK	89	HINES,
. C.D.	48,156	. JAMES K. 110-112
. ROBERT W.	107	. JOSEPH 111
. THOMAS W.		. MAMIE 111
	45,48,106-107	. SUSIE 111
. W.P.	107	HITCHCOCK,
. WALTER	107	. S.M. 36,87
. WILLIAM	54	HODGES, 56
HARLEY,W.I.	53	. H. 128
HARMAN,JOHN	74	. WILLIAM 26,73
. JOHN C.	43,46	HOLLIFIELD 13,28
. WILLIAM	43	. 63,64, 74,141,167
. WILLIAM N.	43	. CLARA 108
HARRIS,19,54,64,115		. H.N. 25,62,70,73,81
. DAN	148	. 102,108,119,140,169
. DAN C.	166	. WILSON L. 102
. EMMIE	152	HOLLIMAN,H.H. 103
. EUGENE	149	HOLMES,E.L. 103
. J.J.	148	. ED 42
. THOMAS	11	. EDWARD A. 94
. THOMAS M.	152,169	HOLT 34
. WALTER	148	HOOD,
. WILEY	30,33	. SHEROD 169
.	138,148	. SIMON 169
HARRISON	57	. WILLIAM 51,167
. DAVID W.	74	HOOK 97
. GREEN B.	57	. EMMIE HARRIS,152
. JOHN G.	57, 147	. J.H. 99
. T.I.	33	. JAMES S. 73,152
HAYES,		HOOKS
. WILLIAM P.	128	. JAMES H. 129
HAYNES,		HORNE 61
. MARIA BROOKINS		HOWELL 70
.	156	. EVAN P. 119
HENDRICKS,	50	HUDGINS,W.T. 88
HERMAN,ISAAC	65	HUFF,JOHN 156
HERMANN		HUNT,WILLIAM 50
. ABE	55,136	HYMAN 103
. ABRAM	135	. J.J. 53,78-79
. HENRY	110,136	. 168-169
. IKE	136	HYMES,

. BENNETT	134
. JENNIE HAPP	134
IRWIN	70
. A.J.	164
. ALEXANDER	10,82
.	105, 167
. ANDREW	11
. FANNIE LOU	165
. FINDLAY	165
. HUGH	11
. JARED	10,43,89
. 105,106,128,166-167	
. JEFF A.	26,100,105
. JOHN	
. LAWSON	105,167
. MARY	
. STEPHENS	164
. T.J.	105
. WILLIAM	10,82
.	105,167
JACKSON	70
. CHARLES	50
. HENRY R.	119
. JOSEPH	50
. MORGAN	120
JACOBSON,	
. CHARLES	45
JEFFERSON,	
. THOMAS	141
JENKINS	
. CHARLES J.	119
JERNIGAN,. A.J.	157
. FANNIE	
. THOMPSON	157
. MACK	81,156
JOHNSON	19,70,104
. JAMES E.	87
. WILLIAM	10,82
JOINER	19,57,104
JONES,BEN	26

INDEX

. MAE	110	. MARY E.	124	. WILLIAM	115
. S.A.H.	70	LECONTE		McCLENDON	
JORDAN	54,62	. JOSEPH	16	. ANNIE	103
	82,111	LEIBERMAN,I.B.	33	McCRARY	
. J.P.	70	LIEBERMAN,I.B.	138	. A.J.	87
. JOHN	49	LOCKHART		McDADE	103
. N.H.	55	. JOHN	122	McDONALD	19
S.G.	81,111,121	LOVETT,B.B.	33	McKENZIE,	
. STEVE J.	170	LUMPKIN	19	. MAE	109
. SUSIE HINES	111	MANSON,ORIAN	130	McPHERSON	19
JOYNER	56	MARSHALL,E.W.	42	NEWMAN	116,153
. CHARLES M.	129	MARTIN	70	. ANN	
. SARAH STUBBS	129	. JOHN	10,82	. AINSWORTH	139
KELLEY	19	MATHIS,A.	144	. H.D.	34
. JACOB	10	. HORACE	80	. I.W.	139
. JAMES	45	MATTHEW		. J.D.	139
. JAMES M.	82	. LEVEN	144	. M.	71
. LAWSON	42	. WILLIAM C.	144	. MARK,	9,86,134,139
. ROBERT	45	MATTHEWS,		NEWS	57
KELLY,LAWSON	45	. ELIZABETH	163	NEWSOME	54,70
. SEABORN	45	. L. CLAYTON	163	NEWTON,JOHN	49
KENDALL,LOULA	46	. W.C.	156	. MOSES	49
KEYES	29	MAY,WILLIAM	10	NUTTE,J.	10
KILPATRICK,		MAYO	30,109	OQUINN,M.N.	58
. WASH	169	. REUBEN	85	ORR	55,104
KING,T.B.	110	MEDLOCK,J.M.G.	81	. T.J.	55
LANG	34,93,96	MEIER,NEAL	56	OSBORNE	
. HENRY	128	MITCHELL,C.H.	81,82	. HENRY	82
. HENRY C.	127	. CHARLIE	169	OVERBY, N.	110
. NANCY DAVIS	127	. E.H.	28	PAGE	53,57
. S.G.	30,122	. LAURA	103	. JAMES A.	53
	127-128	MORGAN,		PARIS	137
. SAMUEL W.	127	. MARTIN	169	. HENRY	136
LANGMADE,E.S.	128	MOSES,ALICE	109	PARK,CLARA	103
. EDWARD	73	. STANFORD E.	146	. WILLIAM	81
LANIER,J.N.	87	. W.M.	101	. WILLIE	103
LAWSON	78,156	. WILLIAM		PARSONS,	
. ALEXANDER	51	. MOULTRIE	44	. CHARLES	150
. ANDREW		McAFEE	56-57	. CHARLES C.	149
. THOMPSON	167	McBRIDE	56	. ELIJAH	149
HUGH	10,29	McCARTY	116	. ELISHA	87
	77-78,142	. W.A.	30,115		

INDEX

PATE	53	. ANDERSON 52
PATKIS, JOHN	49	ROBERTSON,
PEACOCK	57,70	. JOHN 82
. E.S.	57	ROBINSON 19
PEELER, J.E.	58	ROBISON,
PENDLETON, P.C.	80	. ALEX 81
PERRY,		. JOHN W. 81
. MARY WALKER	155	RODGERS 122
PITMAN, NIMROD	168	. R. 128
PITT, WILLIAM	78	. R.L. 26
POPE, OWEN	81,168	. ROBERT L. 19,121
. OWEN C.	80,104	ROGERS,
PRINCE, OLIVER	119	. ELIZ. WILLIAMS 114
PRINGLE	28	. JARED 114
. C.R.	25,30	. JOHN N. 74,170
	117,142,169-170	. LESLIE 113
. NORA		. LOULA KENDALL 46
	BRANTLEY 117	. O.L. 100, 110,112
PRITCHARD		. OSCAR 170
. L.J.	130	. OSCAR H. 113
QUINN	102	. R.L 81
. JOE	92	ROUGHTON, B.E. 28
. JOHN	36	. BRADFORD 169
. JOHN A.	92	. BRADFORD E. 81
. JOHN H.	92	RUDISILL 75
RAWLINGS	19,110	. J.W. 70
. A.A.	93,161	. JOHN W. 74
. ARTHUR A.	161	. RUMPH 100
. B.T.	93,130,156	RUSHIN, JAMES 169
. BEN	93	RUTHERFORD
. BEN T.	150	. JOHN 10-11,82
. C.G.	93	118-119,167
. C.W.	93	SAFFOLD, ISHAM 73
. EZEKIAL	93	SAUNDERS, 18
. FRED	93	. M. 10
. FRED B.	110	SCOTT, WALTER 171
. GEORGE	93	SESSION 104
. WILLIAM	30,93	SESSIONS,
	99,108	. BENJAMIN 50
RENFROE	96	. JOSEPH 50
. J.W.	120	SEWELL,
RIDDLE	53	. WILBUR S. 91

SHAFFORD, JOHN	82
SHEHE, DANIEL	49
SHELNUTT	34,110
. C.D.	36
SHEPPARD	104
. JOHN	10
SHERMAN	16,27,43
.	60,63,65-67,89
. 103-104,111,126,134	
. W.T.	27
SHIELDS, WILLIAM	82
SINQUEFIELD	
. A.	10
. AARON	82
. SAMUEL	82
SKRINE,	
. WILLIAM	68
SMITH	10,19,34
.	56-57,64,96,144
. BELLE	124
. BEN R.	61
. BILLIE	75,124
.	151,156
. BUFORD	51
. COLESBY	50
. HOVEY	161
. I.L.	81
. J.W.	44
. JAMES R.	27,65
.	73,115
. JAMES	
. REMBERT	128
. JOE RICH	44
. JOHN	43,46
. JOHN E.	131
. LEE	61
. LOPEZ	61
. R.L.	161,166
. SALLIE	124,156
. T.N.	44
. T.W.	46
. TOM	44

INDEX

. WILBUR 161
. WILLIAM 73
. WILLIAM HOVEY 30
SNEED,WILLIAM 43
SNELL 56
SPARKS 19
. GEORGE 144
. JOHN 51,167
. THOMAS 92,143
. THOMAS H. 92,143
. THOMAS J. 170
STEPHENS 33
. ALEXANDER H. 121
. JAMES BERRIEN 44
STEWART,
. A.W. 129
. MARY STUBBS 129
STONE,D. 103
STUBBS, ANNIE
  WALLACE 128
. ARCHIE 129
. EDWIN 129
. EMMA 129
. FRANK 129
. GABRIEL 129
. JASPER 129
. JOHN 128-129
. MARGARET 129
. MARTHA 129
. MARY 129
. SARAH 129
. WILLIAM 129
SULLIVAN,
. E.A. 26,28,121,169
SUMMERLIN,
. M.D.C.M. 170
SWINT, THOMAS
. JEFFERSON 86
TALIAFERRO 79
. G.W.H. 169
. LOU
 TARBUTTON 79

. P.R. 74-75
. PATRICK ROSE 126
TANNER
. BEN R. 100,162
. JOHN F. 163
TARBUTTON,B. 51
. B.J 28,36,79,148
. 149,156,158
. BEN 169
. BENJAMIN 73
. LOU 79
. MAMIE BANGS 158
. MARY 164
. SADIE 165
TAYLOR 55
. J.R. 53
. S.J. 88
TENNILLE,B. 10
. BENJAMIN 18,82
. BENJAMINE 41
. FRANCIS 10,49
THIGPEN 54
. C.D. 153
. CHARLES C. 86
. W.R. 114
. WILLIAM R. 85
THOMAS,A.G. 169
. ATTIE 103
. JAMES 82
. JOHN 10
. W.A. 77
THOMPSON 75
. A.C.C. 29,74
. 108,150,157
. CLARA
. HOLLIFIELD 108
. FANNIE 157
TODD,DETT 130
. DOTT 130
TOWNE 19
TROUP

. GEORGE M. 19
TUCKER 19,110
VEAL,O.F. 58
WADLEY
. WILLIAM 127-128
WALKER
. ELIZABETH 76
. W.A. 58
WALL,CHARLES 85
WALLACE,ANNIE 128
WALTERS 19
WARE,A.G. 80
WARREN,W.M. 88
WARTHEN 96,151
. GEORGE D.
. 20,87,149
. LEE 28,148
. MACON 148
. R. LEE 25
. R.L. 147
. RICHARD 20, 21
. T.J. 70,95
. THOMAS
. JEFFERSON 21,125
. W. 10
. WILLIAM 51,129,167
WASHINGTON,
. GEORGE 9
WATTS,JOHN 10-11
WAYNE 70
WELLS,THOMAS 62
. THOMAS F. 70
WEST 64
. EMILY 165-166
WHEELER 63-66
WHITAKER 28,103
. G.W.H. 102
. J.M. 57
WHITE 10,13,16,51
WHITEHEAD,
. MOLLIE 29
WICKER 19,151

INDEX

. ROBERT 10,20
WILKINSON, R. 11
WILLIAMS,
. ELISHA 10,82
. ELIZABETH 114
. JOSHUA 82
. MARVIN 130
. MARY ANN 6,156
WOOD 56-57
. A.W.J. 57,132
. AUGUSTUS 131
. BENJAMIN 131
. CHARLES S. 132
. D. 10
. E. PIERCE 130
. E.P. 165
. ERNEST C. 131
. FRANKLIN 130
. G.H. 131
. GEORGE 129-130
. GORDON C. 130
. HARRY 129
. HENRY H. 130
. HUBERT 129
. J. HINES 130
. J.S. 105,129,132
. JAMES H. 130
. JAMES RAIFORD 57
. JORDAN 130
. M.G. 131
. MARGARET
  STUBBS 129
. MATTHEW K. 131
. MIZEL 131
. MIZEL G. 129-130
. NEWMAN 130
. ROBERT 131
. SAMUEL W. 130
. J. 131
. WADE 74
. WADE H. 57,132
. WILLIAM 131
. WILLIAM T. 130
WYLLY, W.H. 81
YOUNG 57
YOUNGBLOOD
. J.T. 35

www.ingramcontent.com/pod-product-compliance
Lightning Source LLC
Chambersburg PA
CBHW031418290426
44110CB00011B/438